PHRASING

ADVANCED RUDIMENTS FOR
CREATIVE DRUMMING

To access audio visit:
www.halleonard.com/mylibrary

Enter Code
3001-5593-2740-8044

RUSS GOLD

Berklee Press

Editor in Chief: Jonathan Feist
Vice President of Online Learning and Continuing Education: Debbie Cavalier
Assistant Vice President of Operations for Berklee Media: Robert F. Green
Assistant Vice President of Marketing and Recruitment for Berklee Media: Mike King
Dean of Continuing Education: Carin Nuernberg
Editorial Assistants: Matthew Dunkle, Reilly Garrett, Zoë Lustri, José Rodrigo Vazquez
Cover Design: Ranya Karifilly, Small Mammoth Design
Cover Photo: Lincoln Adler
Video Capture: Alex Vo. Editing and Production: Russ Gold
Music Composed and Performed by Russ Gold and Greg Sankovitch

ISBN 978-0-87639-149-5

1140 Boylston Street
Boston, MA 02215-3693 USA
(617) 747-2146

Visit Berklee Press Online at
www.berkleepress.com

Study with

 BERKLEE ONLINE

online.berklee.edu

DISTRIBUTED BY

HAL•LEONARD®
CORPORATION
7777 W. BLUEMOUND RD. P.O. BOX 13819
MILWAUKEE, WISCONSIN 53213

Visit Hal Leonard Online at
www.halleonard.com

Berklee Press, a publishing activity of Berklee College of Music, is a not-for-profit educational publisher.
Available proceeds from the sales of our products are contributed to the scholarship funds of the college.

CONTENTS

VIDEO TRACKS

To access these videos, audio play-along tracks, and some additional notation for the "Drum Set Applications" exercises, go to **www.halleonard.com/mylibrary** and enter the code found on the first page of this book. This will grant you instant access to these files. Examples that include video are marked with icons throughout the book.

Media Extras

ACKNOWLEDGMENTS

I'm deeply grateful to have studied with some of the greatest teachers on the instrument: Gary Chaffee, Alan Dawson, Danny Perez, Steve Bagby, Dave Garibaldi, John Riley, and Bob Moses. These teachers all had a personal and deep understanding of the drums. Their methods inspired my playing, my teaching, and my life.

Personal thanks to my family: Helen and Hal, Sherry, and Steve Gold. My wife Dana.

Thanks to Don Frank at Gelb Music for gear and spiritual support. Thanks to Zildjian for additional gear support.

Thanks to the many students and their families that helped in forming the exercises and concepts in this book: Michael and Cha-Cha Lazerous, Ted and Alan Rice, and Nion McEvoy.

Special thanks to Jonathan Feist and his team at Berklee for their hard work and partnership on this project.

Using Phrases to Build Hand Technique

In many years of studying and practicing the drums, I have found that there is a disconnection between most hand exercises and their real-world application. Most books addressing stick control have a common problem: They present exercises that are based on *sticking patterns* instead of *rhythmic phrases*. These patterns rarely lead to real musical application from a student's practice.

The purpose of this book is to give drummers a vocabulary of simple phrases that become a virtual "Swiss Army Knife" of rhythmic applications. The main tool is the "Essential One-Bar Phrases"—a master list of phrases, which you can find on the back flap of this book. All of the lessons in this book use these one-bar phrases as the skeleton of the exercises. Each phrase has a simple version (a) and a busier version (b). The basic rhythm in (a) has been carried over to (b) with a few added eighth notes so that the "clave" of the phrase remains constant. I've used only four phrases that "permutate" (the same rhythm with shifting start points), so that this limited repertoire opens up great improvisational possibilities. The book is formatted so that you can keep the "Phrase Page" open and visible on the right while you apply the lessons. You will find the first few phrases of each lesson written out so you can see how the exercises correspond to their relative phrase. Go on to apply the exercises to the rest of the phrases on the back flap.

The process of working with this book is that you will play each exercise at least four times through, and then move directly on to the next without stopping. *Repetition* is the student's secret weapon. I've set up this book to produce 92 measures (23 essential phrases, played four times each) of continuous playing for each exercise. This consistent, focused practice will put a workload on your hands and produce noticeable results in short time. I recommend that you count 4-bar phrases aloud for the first few times through. Eventually, you will be able to automatically "feel" 4-bar phrases as you play. That's the goal.

Play the exercises very slowly at first to familiarize yourself with the pattern. Then play them again with the metronome at a slow tempo. Once you have a handle on the shape of the exercise and have it in sync with the metronome, I recommend playing along with music. Anything groove related works well (funk, techno, Afro-Cuban, Caribbean, etc.). Experiment with different feels and tempos. Play the exercises with intensity, just like you are playing in the band. Get inside the music.

The result of the "Phrase" method is that you will develop a roster of phrases ready to play as grooves or in a solo context. You will have a vocabulary that will enable you to speak as freely on the kit as you do talking to your friends. You will express yourself with spontaneity and confidence.

1 Introduction

To access the video, audio, and additional notation that accompanies this book, go to www.halleonard.com/mylibrary and enter the code found on the first page of this book. This will grant you instant access to every example. Where there is a corresponding video, a large video icon is shown, like the one in the margin for the book introduction, track 1. In the "Drum Set Applications," a small icon at the end of a line indicates that a specific step is shown in that video. ▶

Also included on the website are notation examples for each lesson's drum set applications. Print those out, and keep them on hand for reference.

53 Brazilian
Performance
54 Funk Performance
55 Jazz Performance

The accompanying website has three audio play-along tracks that you can use to practice applying the grooves and phrases in this book to real-world situations. You will probably find it most useful to use "Brazilian Play-Along" wherever the baião and samba grooves are referenced, "Jazz Play-Along" wherever jazz grooves are mentioned, and "Funk Play-Along" for any straight-eighth or funk-phrased exercises. For examples of how this might work, you can watch me demonstrate them in the videos "Brazilian Performance," "Funk Performance," and "Jazz Performance."

THE FOUR TYPES OF STICK STROKES

Changes in volume (dynamics) are one of the drummer's tools for telling a rhythmic story and building excitement in a tune. These changes in volume don't come from force, but by changes in stick height. The proper stick stroke is a swing, not a hit. All of the surfaces on a drum kit produce sound by vibrating. Hold the sticks loosely so you can bounce off these vibrating surfaces.

The grip I prefer is a three-point grip between the thumb, index finger, and middle finger. The stick pivots up and down on these three points. Position your hands with the palms facing down and bend at the wrists, swinging the stick loosely from the three points. Be sure to push the stick away from your palm so that the stick has room to swing. Try to keep the stick pinched between your thumb and the first knuckle of your first two fingers. Have a look at the video for a demonstration of the various strokes.

2 The Four Types of Stick Strokes

Here's a rundown of the four strokes used to get the widest dynamic range.

Tap   The stick starts an inch off the pad, drops, and returns an inch off the pad. A soft stroke.

Down   The stick starts at roughly a 90 degree angle from the pad, drops down, and returns to an inch off the pad. This is a loud stroke that comes before a soft stroke.

Up   The stick starts low (1 inch), drops, and snaps up to 90 degrees. It's a soft stroke coming before a loud stoke. Sometimes, the upstroke happens without the tap (snapping up from an inch off the pad).

Full   The stick starts high (90 degrees), comes down, and snaps back up high. A loud stroke.

To learn these strokes, practice the "Essential One-Bar Phrases" (found on the back flap) with all downstrokes, all full strokes, all tap strokes, and all upstrokes.

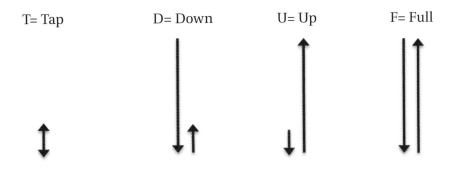

T= Tap   D= Down   U= Up   F= Full

THREE GROOVES

In the "Drum Set Applications" sections that end these lessons, you are frequently asked to play the phrases against three standard grooves: baião, samba, and jazz. Here are the patterns written out. I encourage you to expand your vocabulary with different ride cymbal parts as part of the baião and samba rhythms. In the appendix, you will find these three grooves written out with the 28 essential phrases played on the snare.

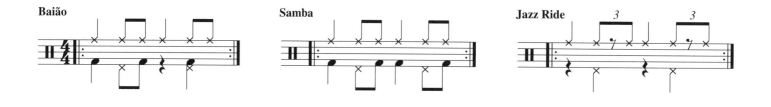

DRUM KEY

This book uses the following notation conventions.

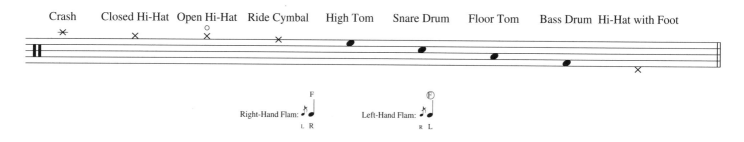

Playing the Phrases along with Quarter Notes

Let's start off by getting familiar with the phrases. These one-bar rhythms are some of the most common used in western music. Pretty much anything that grooves has these phrases tucked into them. Play them slowly on a practice pad, counting eighth notes aloud.

After getting comfortable with where the notes fall, play quarter notes with either your right or left foot while playing the phrases. The vital element to a strong groove is the ability to feel the quarter-note pulse while you play. This will bring your band together and have toes tapping. Remember: what you focus on is what people hear. All great musicians have an internal reference pulse that propels their playing. The stronger your internal pulse, the freer you can be with time and phrasing.

Here are the first eight phrases written out as examples. Play the rest of the exercises looking at the "Essential One-Bar Phrases" page. Once you're comfortable playing these on the practice pad, move on to the "Drum Set Applications."

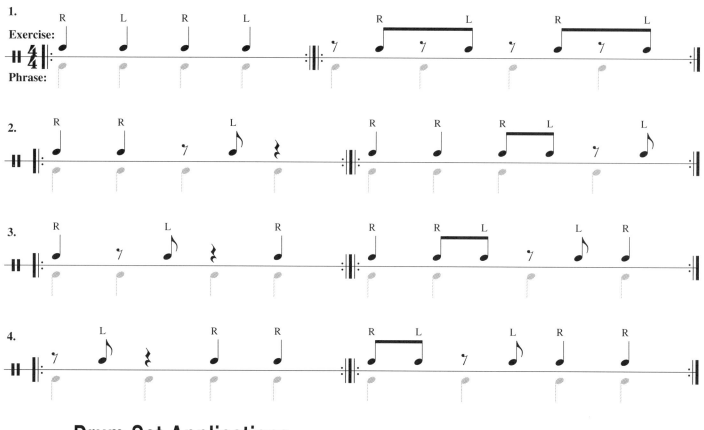

Drum Set Applications

1. Play the phrases as fills around the kit over the bass drum playing quarter notes.

2. Play phrases on the bass drum, eighth notes on hi-hat (RH), and beats 2 and 4 on the snare drum (LH).

3. Play the phrases on the snare drum (LH) and baião or samba (see the introduction) on the bass drum, hi-hat, or ride cymbal.

4. Play the phrases on hi-hat (RH), beats 1 and 3 on the bass drum, and beats 2 and 4 on the snare drum (LH).

5. Play the phrases on the snare drum (LH), jazz ride (RH), and beats 2 and 4 on the hi-hat (LF).

6. Play the phrases on the bass drum, jazz pattern on the ride cymbal (RH), and beats 2 and 4 on the hi-hat (LF).

7. Play the phrases on the bass drum and snare (LH) alternating notes, jazz pattern on the ride cymbal (RH), and hi-hat on beats 2 and 4 (LF).

Below, the drum set applications for lesson 1 are written out, to help you get started with this method. (The numbers in the notation refer to each application, 2A and 2B respectively.) Our first goal is to get familiar with the practice pad exercises, internalize them, and then apply them to the drum set. Practice the exercises slowly, and see where the notes correspond to the foot patterns. After learning a few of the exercises on the practice pad, you will find it easier to transfer all of them to the kit. By learning the patterns on the kit without notation, you will own the rhythms and be able to make music with them!

In the appendix, you will find the "Essential One-Bar Phrases" written out along with the samba, baião, and jazz grooves. Use this to help navigate the relationships between the exercises, the phrases, and the grooves.

If you need further help, drum set applications for each lesson are included on the website. Print them out!

Eighth Notes with Phrase Accents

In this lesson, we will play the phrases as accents within a string of eighth notes. We'll take each phrase and fill in the spaces with eighth notes. The top system shows how the phrases are expressed as accents. The bottom system refers to the corresponding rhythms on the "Essential One-Bar Phrases" page. Play these slowly at first, paying close attention to the stick height information indicated above the notes. At first, go super slow to learn the moves. The goal is to produce physical habits. At the slower speed, you can't really see the whole picture, but be patient. Soon you will get a feel for the patterns and they will become second nature. It's important that for accurate, *relaxed* playing, you focus on stick heights. Similar to tennis, the sooner you bring the racket back, the smoother the swing.

Whenever you see two symbols per note (for example "TU"), it means that both hands move on that note. The first symbol is what the left hand does (tap); the second is what the right hand does (up).

This is a great exercise that has a thousand and one uses. It can be done with either straight eighths or "swing" jazz eighths (see page 26 for an explanation of "swing phrasing").

Play each phrase at least eight times without stopping, and then go directly on to the next. Use a metronome once you feel comfortable with the patterns.

Here are the first eight phrases written out as examples. Play the rest of the exercises looking at the "Essential One-Bar Phrases" page. Once you're comfortable playing these on the practice pad, move on to the "Drum Set Applications."

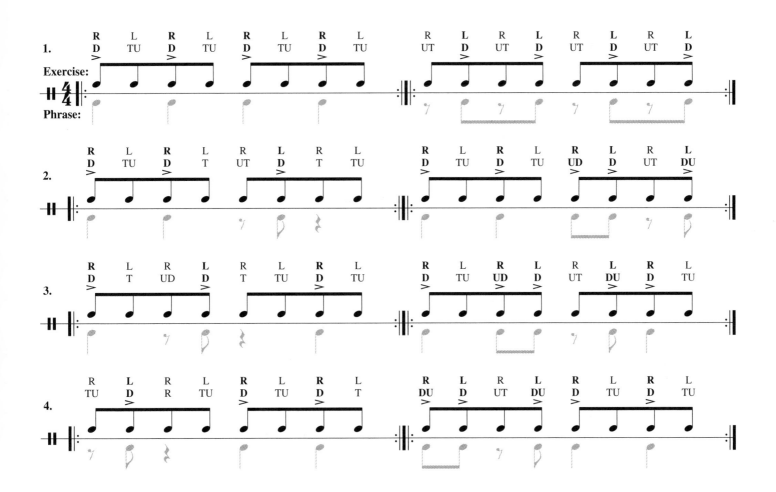

Drum Set Applications

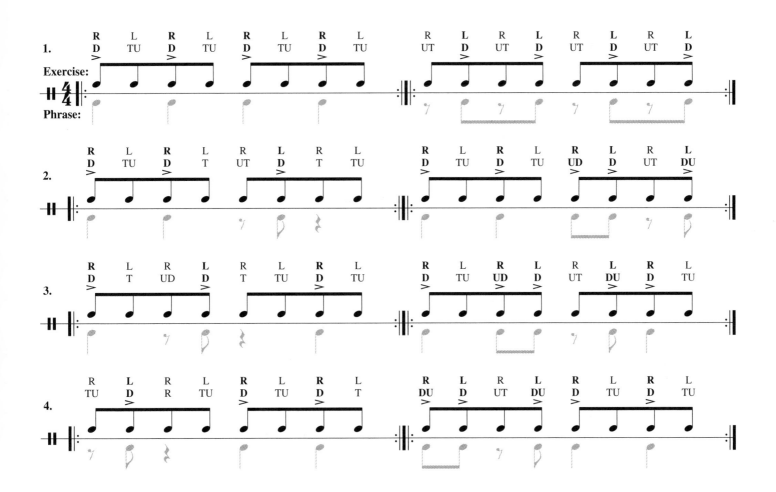

1. Play the exercises on the snare over baião or samba with the feet.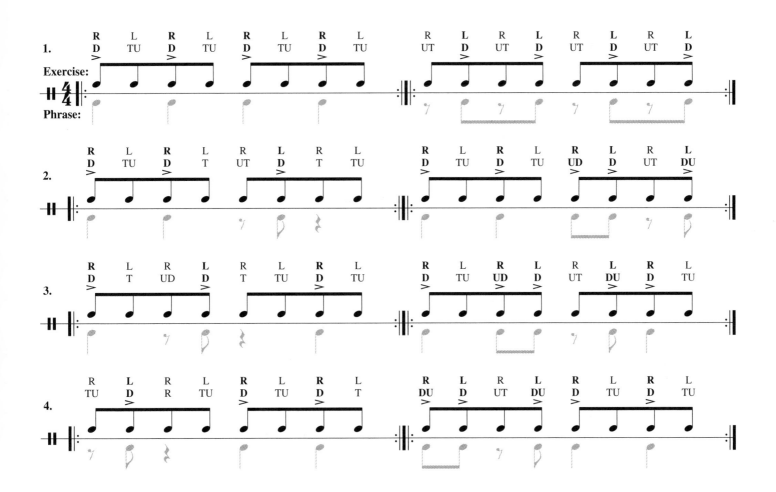

2. Play accented notes on the toms, unaccented notes on the snare, and baião or samba with the feet.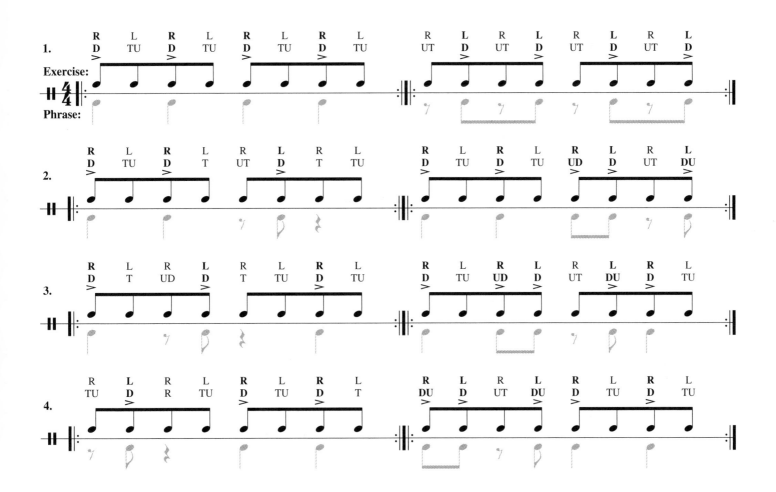

3. Play accented notes as cymbal crashes along with the bass drum, unaccented notes on the snare, and quarter notes on the hi-hat (LF).

4. Play accented notes in unison on the snare drum and floor tom, the bass drum on unaccented notes, and hi-hat quarter notes.

5. Play accented notes with alternating hands on snare drum (LH) and floor tom (RH), the bass drum on the unaccented notes, and hi-hat quarter notes.

6. Play eighth notes on the hi-hat (RH), bass drum on beats 1 and 3, and snare drum on beats 2 and 4 (LH). Play accents as open hi-hat notes.

LESSON 3

Phrase Accents with Double-Stroke Sticking

Play the same accent rhythms from lesson 2 with double-stroke sticking.

Here are the first eight phrases written out as examples. Play the rest of the exercises looking at the "Essential One-Bar Phrases" page. Once you're comfortable playing these on the practice pad, move on to the "Drum Set Applications."

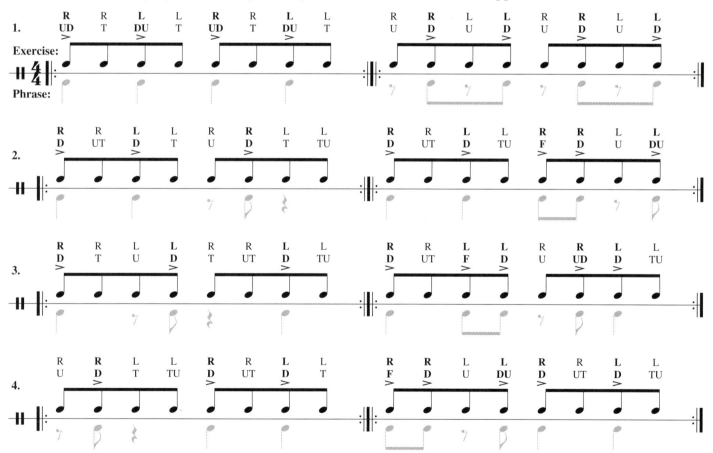

Drum Set Applications

1. Play the exercises on the snare drum over baião or samba with the feet.

2. Play accented notes on the toms, unaccented notes on the snare, and baião or samba with the feet.

LESSON 4

Phrase Accents with Paradiddle Sticking

Now we'll play the accented rhythm from lesson 2 with paradiddle sticking.

Here are the first eight phrases written out as examples. Play the rest of the exercises looking at the "Essential One-Bar Phrases" page. Once you're comfortable playing these on the practice pad, move on to the "Drum Set Applications."

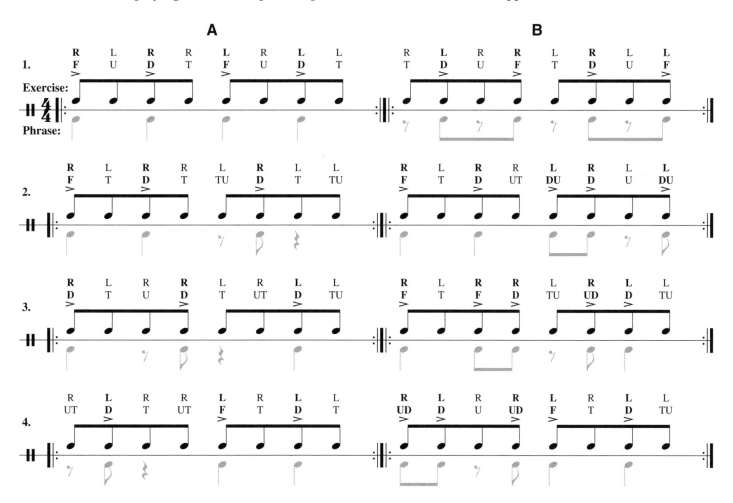

Drum Set Applications

1. Play the exercises on the snare drum over baião or samba with the feet.

2. Play accented notes on the toms, unaccented notes on the snare, and baião or samba with the feet.

Eighth Notes with Phrases in the Right Hand, Left Hand Filling In

In this exercise, we will play the phrase notes with the right hand and fill the eighth notes with the left. Play all the notes evenly with consistent volume. No accents!

Repetition is the key. Play each exercise at least four times before moving on to the next one. Use a metronome. Don't stop until you've gotten to the end of the page.

For an excellent workout that will increase your jazz vocabulary, practice these with swing phrasing.

Here are the first eight phrases written out as examples. Play the rest of the exercises looking at the "Essential One-Bar Phrases" page. Once you're comfortable playing these on the practice pad, move on to the "Drum Set Applications."

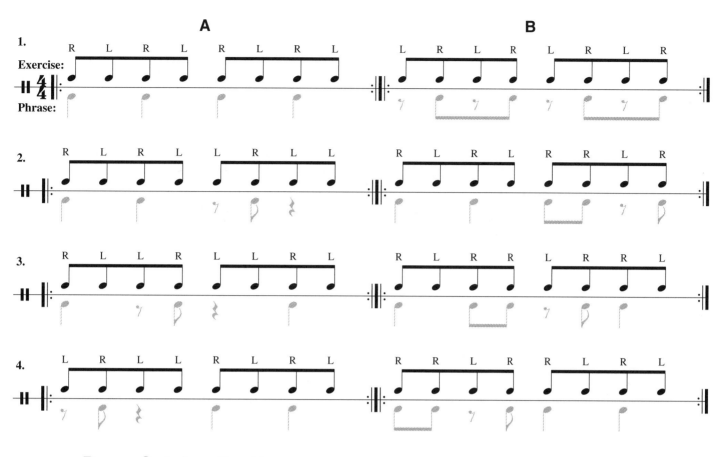

Drum Set Applications

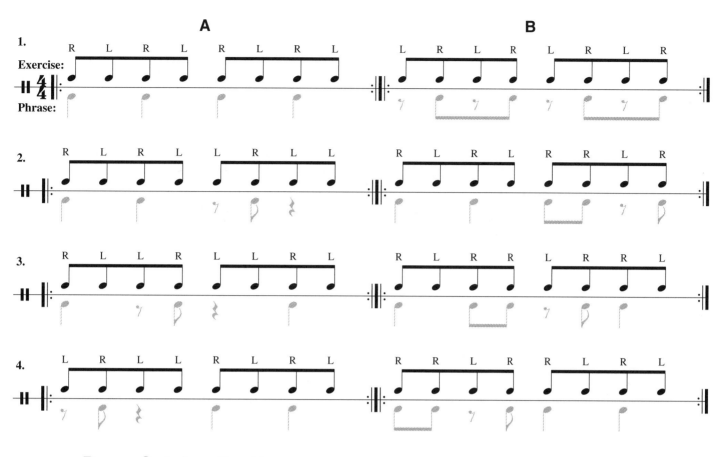

1. Play the exercises on the snare over baião or samba with the feet.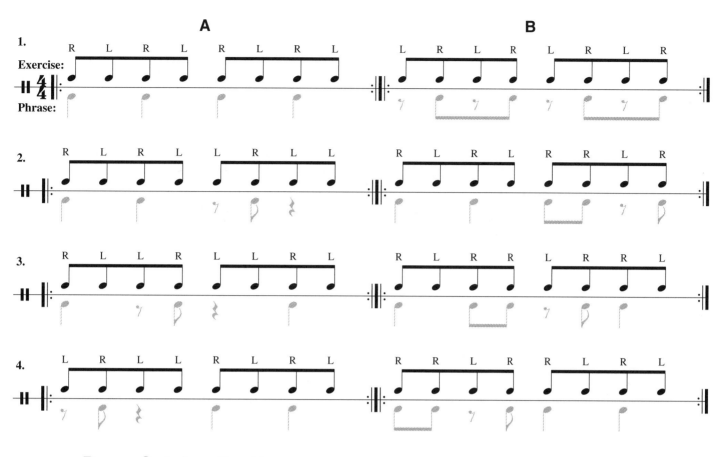

2. Play the exercises on the floor tom (RH) and snare (LH), and baião or samba with the feet.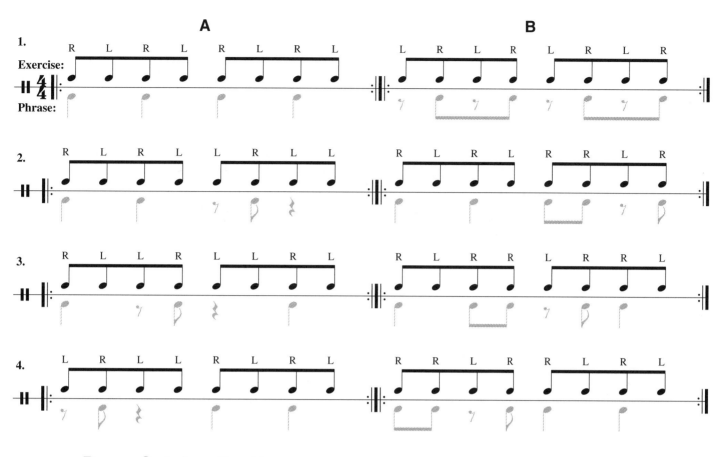

3. Play the phrases on the ride cymbal (RH) with snare drum filling in the eighth notes (LH), bass drum unison with ride, and quarter notes (LF).

4. Play the "R" notes on the bass drum, "L" notes on the snare (LH), and eighth notes on the hi-hat (RH).

5. Play the "R" notes on the bass drum, "L" notes on the snare (LH), the jazz ride pattern (RH), and beats 2 and 4 on the hi-hat (LF). All eighth notes swing.

6. Play the phrase notes on snare, the notes in between alternating bass drum and hi-hat (LH), with the jazz ride-cymbal pattern (RH). Swing the eighth notes.

7. Play the phrase notes on bass drum, the in between notes alternating snare drum and hi-hat (LH), with jazz ride-cymbal pattern (RH). Swing the eighth notes.

8. Play the phrase notes on hi-hat, the in between notes alternating snare drum and bass drum, with the jazz ride-cymbal pattern (RH). Swing the eighth notes.

Doubling the Unaccented Eighths 1: Double Strokes

This technique will help build speed and control by doubling the notes between the phrase notes. We are going to do this three different ways. The first exercise uses double strokes (diddles) to produce the sixteenth notes.

Here are the first eight phrases written out as examples. Play the rest of the exercises looking at the "Essential One-Bar Phrases" page. Once you're comfortable playing these on the practice pad, move on to the "Drum Set Applications."

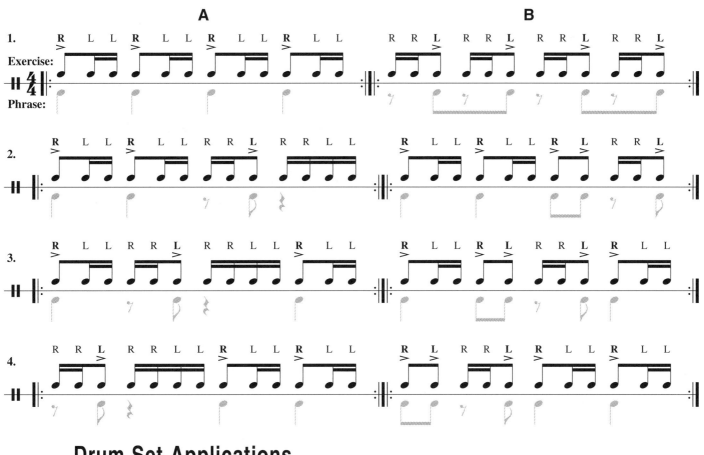

Drum Set Applications

1. Play the exercise on snare over baião or samba with the feet.

2. Play accented notes on the toms, unaccented notes on the snare, and baião or samba with the feet.

3. Play accented notes as cymbal crashes along with bass drum, unaccented notes on the snare, and quarter notes on the hi-hat (LF).

4. Play the exercises half time on the ride cymbal as the jazz ride pattern (RH), with beats 2 and 4 on hi-hat.

5. Add snare, bass drum, or hi-hat in the "holes" after the eighth notes. You can play single hits, buzzed notes, or the second and third partials of a triplet.

Doubling the Unaccented Eighths 2: Alternating Strokes

In this exercise, we'll play the same technique of doubling the unaccented notes but now using alternating strokes. Notice that after exercise 1, the sticking turns around on the repeat. The first time through, start with the right-hand lead. The second time, start with the left, etc. Make sure your unaccented notes are low tap strokes and your accented notes are from high downstrokes.

Here are the first eight phrases written out as examples. Play the rest of the exercises looking at the "Essential One-Bar Phrases" page. Once you're comfortable playing these on the practice pad, move on to the "Drum Set Applications."

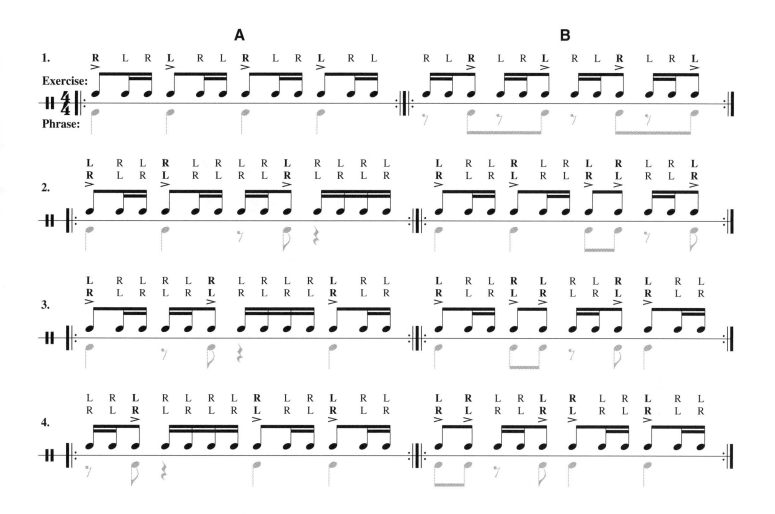

Drum Set Applications

1. Play the exercise on the snare drum over baião or samba with the feet.

2. Play accented notes on the toms, unaccented notes on the snare, and baião or samba with the feet.

3. Play accented notes as cymbal crashes along with bass drum, unaccented notes on the snare, and quarter notes on the hi-hat (LF).

4. Play all notes on various drums as fills, changing drums on the accented notes.

Doubling the Unaccented Eighths 3: Alternating Strokes/Right-Hand Lead

The last of these three exercises is a real workout. The right hand plays all the eighth notes, and the left fills the sixteenths around them. Once you play through with right-hand lead, please switch the sticking to left-hand lead.

Here are the first eight phrases written out as examples. Play the rest of the exercises looking at the "Essential One-Bar Phrases" page. Once you're comfortable playing these on the practice pad, move on to the "Drum Set Applications."

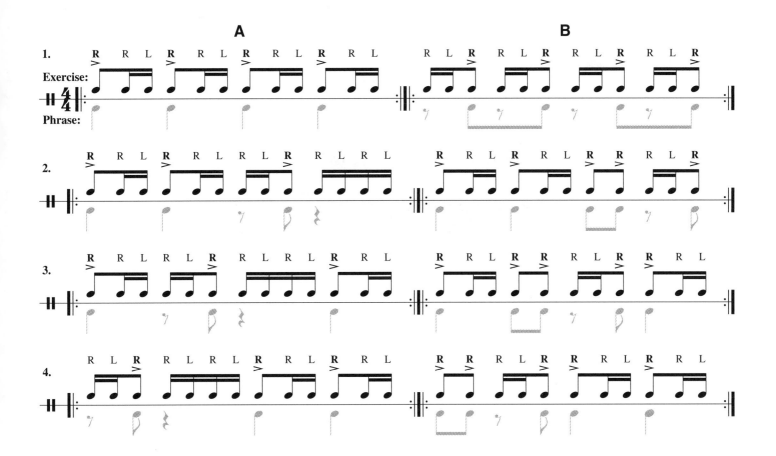

Drum Set Applications

1. Play the exercises on the snare drum over baião or samba with the feet.

2. Play accented notes on the toms, unaccented notes on the snare, and baião or samba with the feet.

3. Play accented notes as cymbal crashes along with bass drum, unaccented notes on the snare, and quarter notes on the hi-hat (LF).

LESSON 9

Triplet on the
Unaccented Eighths

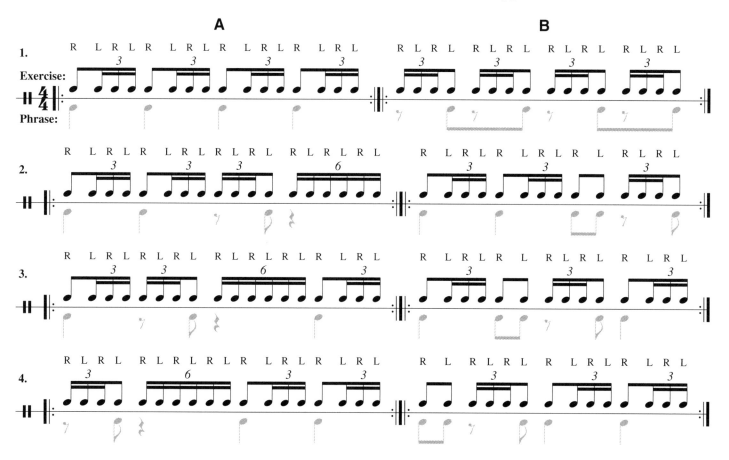

In this exercise, we will play a sixteenth-note triplet on each unaccented eighth note. Try to play all the notes with equal volume—no accents on the phrase notes. Exercise 2A is similar to a bolero.

Here are the first eight phrases written out as examples. Play the rest of the exercises looking at the "Essential One-Bar Phrases" page. Once you're comfortable playing these on the practice pad, move on to the "Drum Set Applications."

Drum Set Applications

1. Play the exercises on the snare drum over baião or samba with the feet.

2. Play phrase notes on the toms, triplet notes on snare, and baião or samba with the feet.

3. Play phrase notes as cymbal crashes along with bass drum, unaccented notes on the snare, and quarter notes on the hi-hat (LF).

LESSON 10

Flams on the Phrases

A flam is two notes played slightly offset from one another. Technically, it's a lightly tapped grace note followed closely by a downstroke with the opposite hand. The effect is two notes producing one fat note. Make sure the notes aren't so close together that you can't hear both!

In these exercises, we'll drill flams by playing them on the phrase note while filling around them with eighth notes. It's important that the grace notes and tap strokes are all low to the pad, and the primary downstroke of the flam starts high up.

Here are the first eight phrases written out as examples. Play the rest of the exercises looking at the "Essential One-Bar Phrases" page. Once you're comfortable playing these on the practice pad, move on to the "Drum Set Applications."

Drum Set Applications

1. Play the exercises on the snare drum over baião or samba with the feet.

2. Play primary flam notes on the toms, unaccented notes on the snare, and baião or samba with the feet.

3. Play primary flam notes with cymbal crashes and bass drum, unaccented notes on the snare, and hi-hat quarter notes (LF).

Oakland Flams

This fun exercise mimics the drumming of the great Oakland drummer Dave Garibaldi. Play the phrases with your right hand, and use the left hand to fill in. Every time there are two consecutive right strokes, play a flam on the first note. Repeat the exercises with the left hand playing the phrases and the right hand filling in.

The phrases produced here are in the style of the grooves Dave played with the group Tower of Power. This exercise only uses the "B" phrases.

Here are six phrases written out as examples. Play the rest of the exercises looking at the "Essential One-Bar Phrases" page. Once you're comfortable playing these on the practice pad, move on to the "Drum Set Applications."

Drum Set Applications

▶

1. Play the exercise on the snare over baião or samba with the feet. ▶

2. Play right hand on hi-hat, left hand on snare drum, and samba or baião with the feet. ▶

3. Play right hand on hi-hat, left hand on snare drum. Bass drum plays unison with the right hand, but leaving out the first of two consecutive eighth notes (right-hand lead). ▶

   • Add open hi-hat unison with bass drum.

4. Play right hand on hi-hat, left hand on snare. Bass drum plays "in the holes" between snare hits (left-hand lead). ▶

   • Add open hi-hat on the second of two consecutive hi-hat hits.

Drags and Drag-Taps

A *drag* is like a three-note flam. The two grace notes have no rhythmic value of their own. They piggyback onto the primary stroke. You'll often hear drags on the snare in soul and funk grooves. It's like sauce between the notes. Place the two grace notes as close to the primary stroke as possible. Note that the ruff is on the phrase note and the accent is played on the eighth note following it. After exercise 1, the sticking alternates with each repeat.

Here are the first eight phrases written out as examples. Play the rest of the exercises looking at the "Essential One-Bar Phrases" page. Once you're comfortable playing these on the practice pad, move on to the "Drum Set Applications."

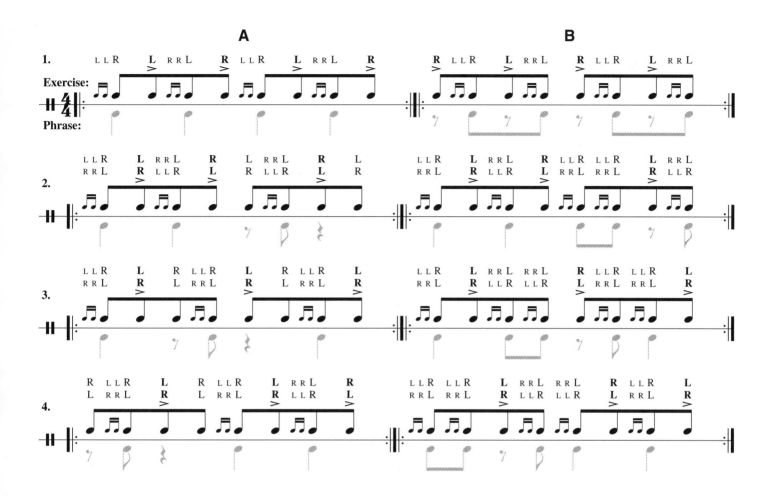

Drum Set Applications

1. Play the exercise on snare over baião or samba with the feet.

2. Play accented notes on the toms, unaccented notes on the snare, and baião or samba with the feet.

3. Play accented notes as cymbal crashes along with bass drum, unaccented notes on the snare, and quarter notes on the hi-hat (LF).

4. Play the exercise on the snare with grace notes on the bass drum.

Four-Stroke Ruffs

Here, we place three grace notes before the primary stroke. Big-band jazz drummers will often play four-stroke ruffs as setups for ensemble hits. Four-stroke ruffs have a ton of energy. Like the flam and drag, the grace notes in the four-stroke ruff have no rhythmic value. They are played the same no matter the tempo of the exercise.

Make sure the three grace notes are soft and relaxed. The primary stroke should be nice and strong. Start slow.

Here are the first eight phrases written out as examples. Play the rest of the exercises looking at the "Essential One-Bar Phrases" page. Once you're comfortable playing these on the practice pad, move on to the "Drum Set Applications."

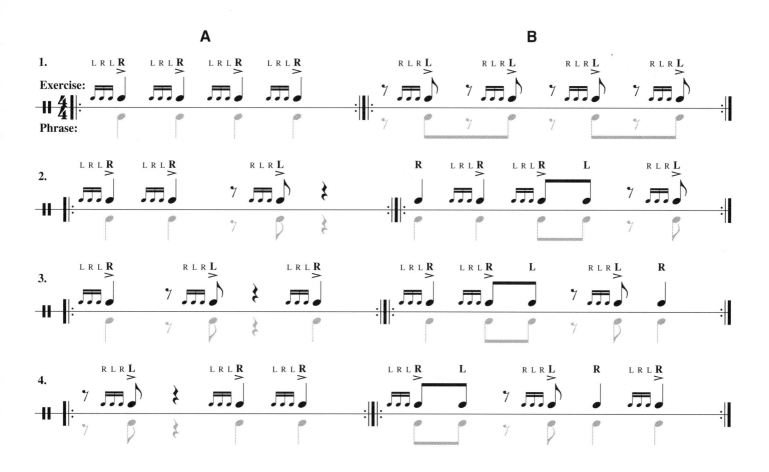

Drum Set Applications

1. Play the exercises on the snare drum over baião or samba with the feet.

2. Play accented notes on the toms, unaccented notes on the snare, and baião or samba with the feet.

3. Play accented notes as cymbal crashes along with bass drum, unaccented notes on the snare, and quarter notes on the hi-hat (LF).

4. Play "Bonham" fills on grace notes (snare/high tom/floor), bass drum on primary notes, snare on the single note that follows the ruff, and quarter notes on the hi-hat (LF).

Triplet with Accents: Alternating Sticking

SWING (JAZZ) EIGHTHS

The rhythm of jazz is based on triplets. There are no even (straight) eighths! This means that eighth notes are altered a bit so that the off-beat eighth notes (the notes between the downbeats) are played a bit late, so that they happen on the last note of a triplet. That's called a "swing feel." It breaks down like this:

In this exercise, we'll look at filling in the triplets around the "swing" phrase notes. This approach shifts the off-beat note a bit later so that it falls on the last note of the triplet. That's swinging, jazz phrasing. It gives the eighth notes a bouncy, loping feel.

The accents are produced by stick height, not by force! The unaccented notes (taps) are played super close to the pad, while the up and down strokes (for the accents) snap all the way up to 90 degrees. Interestingly, it's the *unaccented* notes that are important, not the accented ones. Focus on keeping them soft and consistent.

Here are the first eight phrases written out as examples. Play the rest of the exercises looking at the "Essential One-Bar Phrases" page. Once you're comfortable playing these on the practice pad, move on to the "Drum Set Applications."

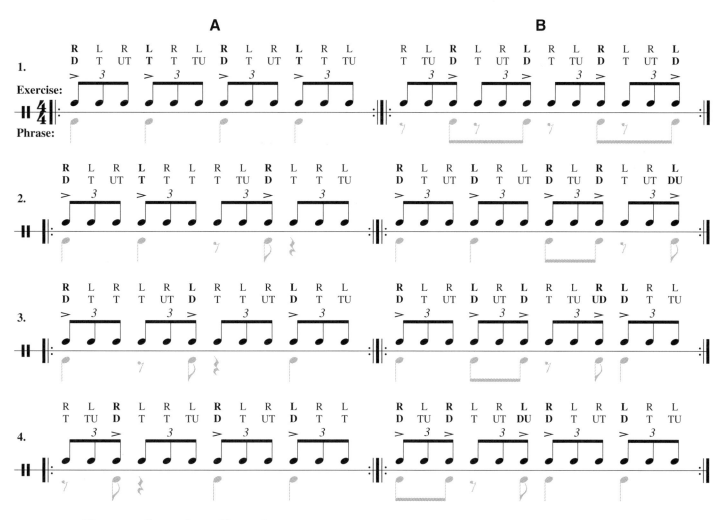

Drum Set Applications

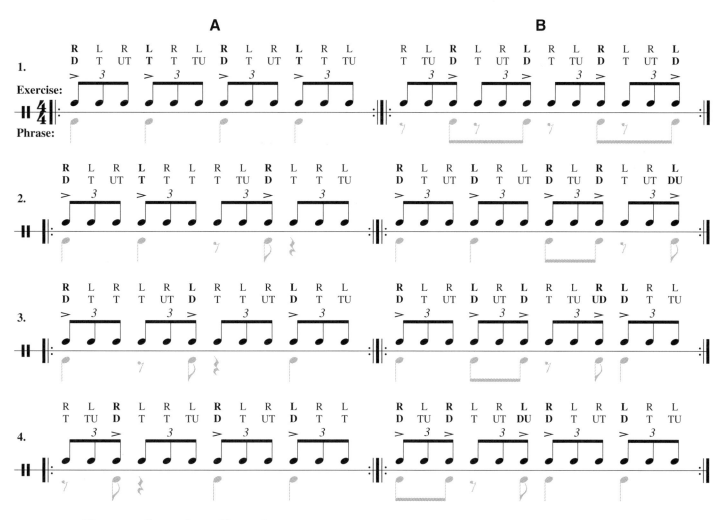

1. Play the exercises on the snare over baião with the feet. Swing the "and" of beat 3 on the bass drum.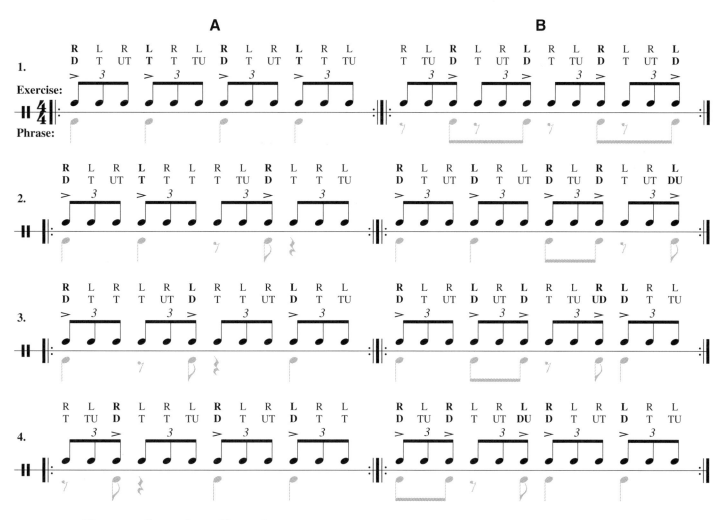

2. Play accented notes on the toms, unaccented on the snare, and baião with the feet.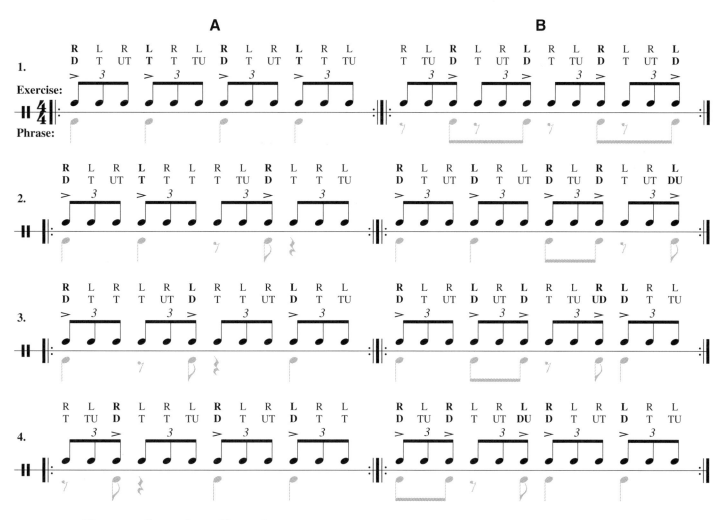

3. Play accented notes on snare, unaccented notes on the toms, and baião with the feet.

4. Play accented notes on crashes along with bass drum, unaccented notes on the snare drum, and beats 2 and 4 on the hi-hat (LF).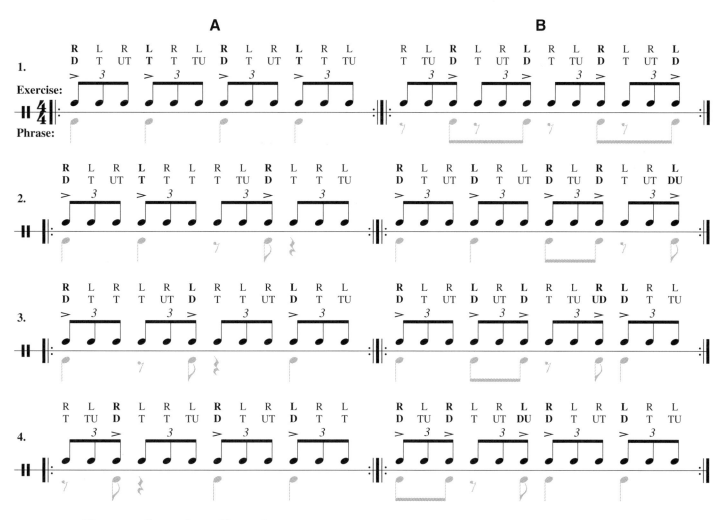

5. "Afro-Pop Style." Play accented notes on the snare drum, unaccented notes on the hi-hat, and quarter notes on the bass drum. Accent the hi-hat note before the snare hit.

6. Play the exercise on the hi-hat (including the accented notes) with the note before each accented note played on the snare. Play the bass drum unison with the right-hand accents.

Filling In with Triplets 1: Right Hand Plays the Phrase, Left Hand Fills In

This exercise is a great way to explore what the left hand can do to support the right-hand phrasing in the swing context. This technique is great for jazz playing or soloing, and there are some fantastic drummers who've used this as part of their signature sound. Elvin Jones and Steve Gadd are a great place to start.

This lesson starts with exercises 1a and 1b, and then continues with only the "b" version phrases.

Here are the first eight phrases written out as examples. Play the rest of the exercises looking at the "Essential One-Bar Phrases" page. Once you're comfortable playing these on the practice pad, move on to the "Drum Set Applications."

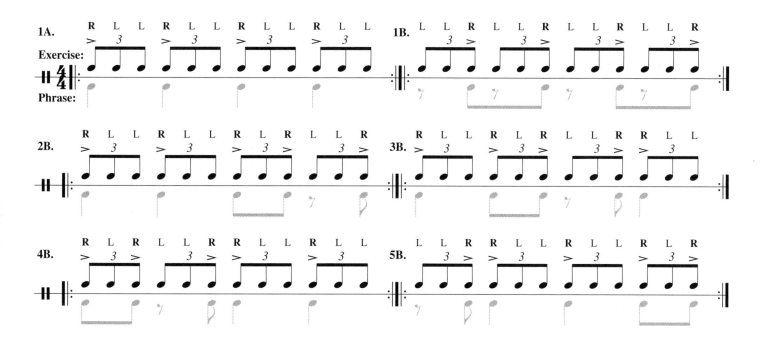

Drum Set Applications

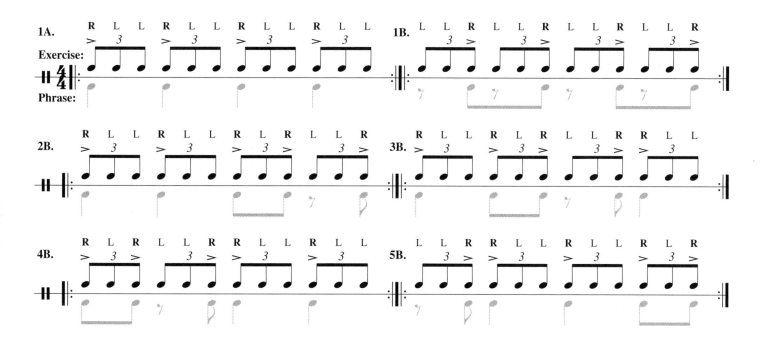

1. Play the exercises on the snare drum over baião with the feet. Swing the "and" of beat 3 on the bass drum. ▶

2. Play accented notes on the toms, unaccented notes on the snare, and baião with the feet. ▶

3. Play accented notes on the crashes along with bass drum, unaccented notes on the snare drum, and beats 2 and 4 on the hi-hat (LF). ▶

4. Play the jazz ride-cymbal pattern (RH), accented notes on the bass drum, unaccented notes on the snare drum, and beats 2 and 4 on hi-hat (LF). ▶

5. Play the jazz ride-cymbal pattern (RH), accented notes on snare drum, unaccented notes on bass drum, and beats 2 and 4 on hi-hat (LF). ▶

6. Play accented notes on the bass drum, alternate hands on the unaccented notes (RH floor tom, LH snare drum), and hi-hat on quarter notes (LF). ▶

7. Play accented notes with both hands together and unaccented notes on the bass drum, and hi-hat on quarter notes (LF). ▶

LESSON 16

Filling In with Triplets 2: Left Hand Plays the Phrase, Right Hand Fills In

This is like lesson 15 but starting with the left hand.

Here are the first six phrases written out as examples. Play the rest of the exercises looking at the "Essential One-Bar Phrases" page. Once you're comfortable playing these on the practice pad, move on to the "Drum Set Applications."

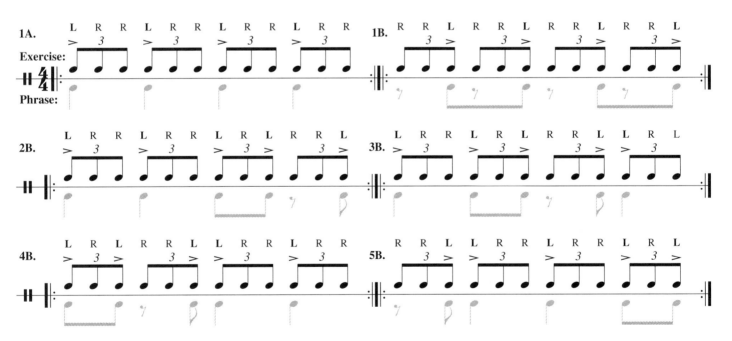

Drum Set Applications

1. Play exercises on the snare over baião with the feet. Swing the "and" of beat 3 on the bass drum.

2. Play with accented notes on the toms, unaccented notes on the snare, and baião with the feet.

3. Play accented notes on the crashes along with bass drum, unaccented notes on the snare drum, and beats 2 and 4 on the hi-hat (LF).

LESSON 17

Filling In with Triplets 3: "Switchies"

This is a fun way to combine right-hand and left-hand leads. We'll start this exercise with the right hand playing the accents, left hand filling in. When we come to two accents in a row, switch to left-hand lead. Keep switching leads as you repeat the exercise. This lesson uses only the "B" phrases.

Here are the first four phrases written out as examples. Play the rest of the exercises looking at the "Essential One-Bar Phrases" page. Once you're comfortable playing these on the practice pad, move on to the "Drum Set Applications."

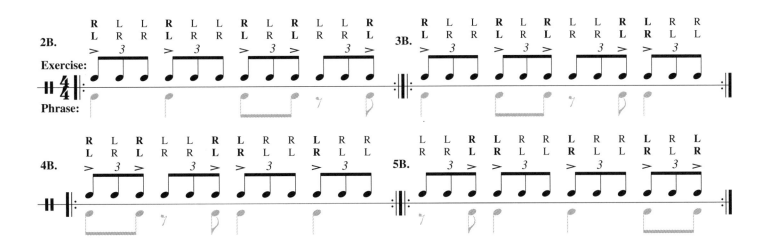

Drum Set Applications

1. Play the exercises on the snare drum over baião with the feet. Swing the "and" of beat 3 on the bass drum.

2. Play with accented notes on the toms, unaccented notes on the snare, and baião with the feet.

3. Play accented notes on the crashes along with bass drum, unaccented notes on the snare, and beats 2 and 4 on the hi-hat (LF).

4. Play the jazz ride-cymbal pattern (RH), bass drum on "R" notes, snare drum on "L" notes, and beats 2 and 4 on the hi-hat (LF).

LESSON 18

Ratamacues

Here are examples of the single and double ratamacue. As you play this rudiment, be sure to keep the speed of the triplet accurate. Take care to keep the ruff tucked up close to the start of the triplet.

Single Ratamacue:

R R L R L R
L L R L R L

Double Ratamacue:

L L R L L R L R L
R R L R R L R L R

Ratamacues and Double Ratamacues on the Phrases

In this exercise, we'll use a ruff followed by sixteenth-note triplets to fill in the space between phrase notes. This is a great chops buster! Start slow, and be sure to play only two taps per ruff stroke. Note that starting with number 2, these exercises alternate lead when you hit the repeat.

Here are the first eight phrases written out as examples. Play the rest of the exercises looking at the "Essential One-Bar Phrases" page. Once you're comfortable playing these on the practice pad, move on to the "Drum Set Applications."

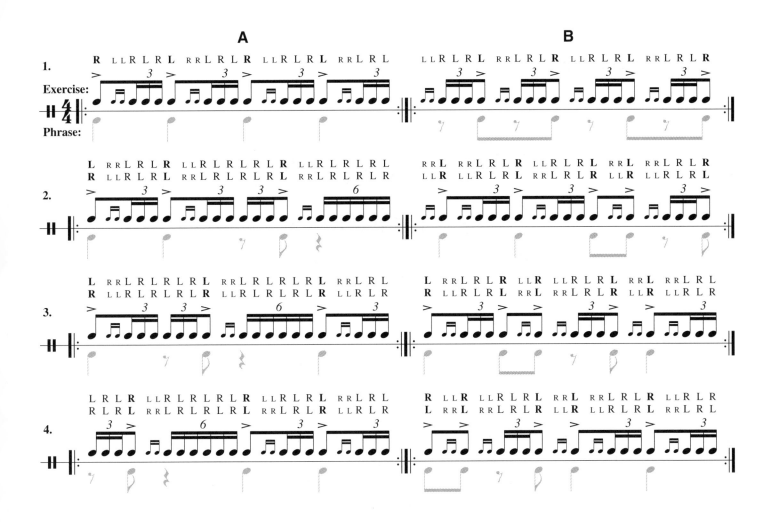

Drum Set Applications

1. Play the exercises on the snare drum over baião or samba with the feet.

2. Play accented notes on the toms, unaccented notes on the snare, and baião or samba with the feet.

3. Play accented notes as cymbal crashes along with bass drum, unaccented notes on the snare, and beats 2 and 4 on the hi-hat (LF).

4. Play the exercise on the snare drum with grace notes on the bass drum.

LESSON 20

Triplets with Unaccented Notes Doubled: Double Strokes

In this lesson, we take the triplets between the phrase notes and double them. The hands move at the same rate but play two taps on impact instead of one (diddle). Once you get into this, you will start to recognize these phrases in the work of Mitch Mitchell, Buddy Rich, and Mel Lewis.

Here are the first eight phrases written out as examples. Play the rest of the exercises looking at the "Essential One-Bar Phrases" page. Once you're comfortable playing these on the practice pad, move on to the "Drum Set Applications."

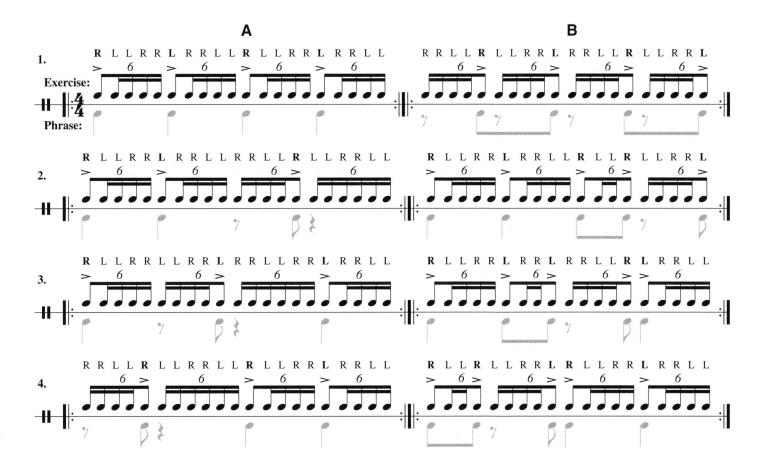

Drum Set Applications

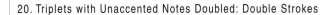

1. Play the exercises on the snare drum over baião with the feet. Swing the "and" of 3 on the bass drum. ▶

2. Play with accented notes on the toms, unaccented notes on the snare, and baião with the feet. ▶

3. Play accented notes on the crashes along with bass drum, unaccented notes on snare drum, and beats 2 and 4 on the hi-hat (LF). ▶

Triplets with Unaccented Notes Doubled: Alternating Strokes

This is like lesson 20 but with the doubled notes played as alternating strokes. It's a bit harder (hands move faster!) and has a more driving sound. These are an additional challenge in that after exercise 1, they turn around on the repeat: first time through right-hand lead; second time through left-hand lead. As always, speed comes with slow and relaxed practice.

Here are the first eight phrases written out as examples. Play the rest of the exercises looking at the "Essential One-Bar Phrases" page. Once you're comfortable playing these on the practice pad, move on to the "Drum Set Applications."

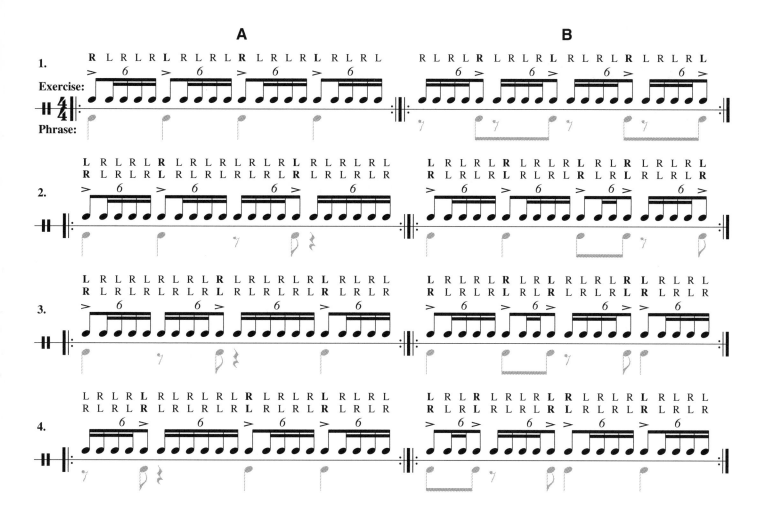

Drum Set Applications

1. Play the exercises on the snare drum over baião with the feet. Swing the "and" of 3 on the bass drum.

2. Play with accented notes on the toms, unaccented notes on the snare, and baião with the feet.

3. Play accented notes on the crashes along with bass drum, unaccented notes on the snare, and beats 2 and 4 on the hi-hat (LF).

Triplets with Flams

Now we'll take the same triplet exercise and play flams on the accented notes. They alternate all the way through.

Be sure to keep all of the strokes *low to the pad* except the downstroke of the flam. In other words, the right stroke of the right flam comes from up high and ends down low after striking the pad. Everything else is a tap stroke.

Here are the first eight phrases written out as examples. Play the rest of the exercises looking at the "Essential One-Bar Phrases" page. Once you're comfortable playing these on the practice pad, move on to the "Drum Set Applications."

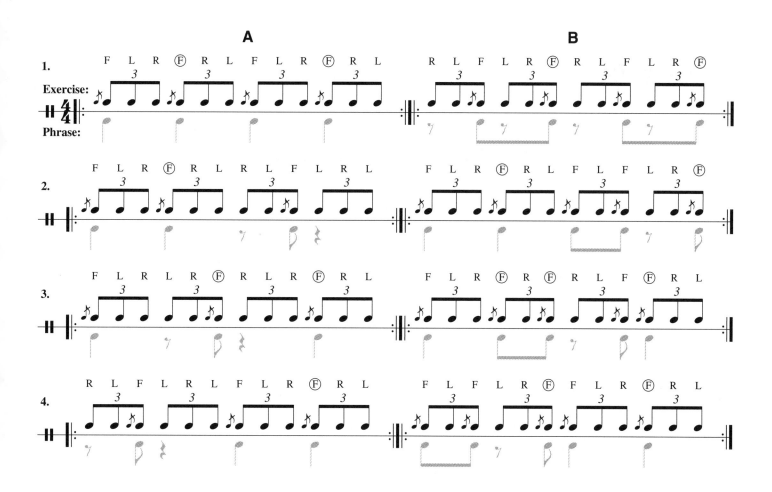

Drum Set Applications

1. Play the exercises on the snare drum over baião with the feet. Swing the "and" of 3 on the bass drum. ▶

2. Play primary flam notes on the toms, everything else on the snare, and baião with the feet. ▶

3. Play primary flam notes on the crashes along with bass drum, everything else on the snare, and beats 2 and 4 on the hi-hat (LF). ▶

Filling in the Phrases with Sixteenth Notes

Here, we get to fill in the space with sixteenth notes. Play slowly, and swing the stick back on the sixteenth before the accented notes. Once you've played these with right-hand lead, go back and play them starting with the left! These phrases work really well as rock fills.

Here are the first eight phrases written out as examples. Play the rest of the exercises looking at the "Essential One-Bar Phrases" page. Once you're comfortable playing these on the practice pad, move on to the "Drum Set Applications."

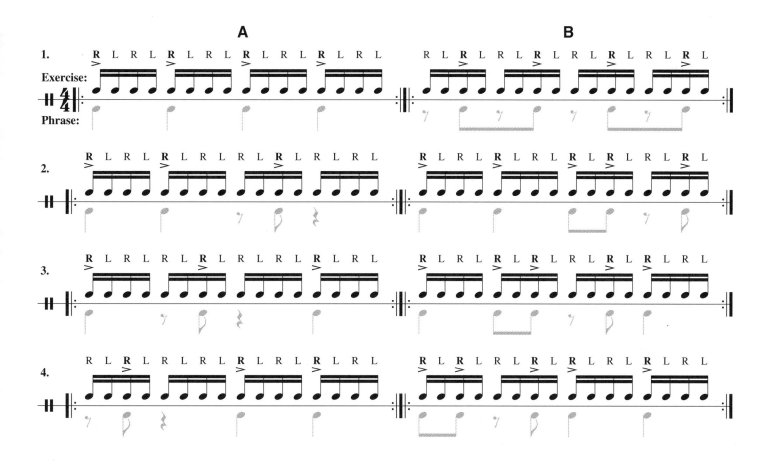

Drum Set Applications

1. Play the exercises on the snare drum over baião or samba with the feet.

2. Play accented notes on the toms, unaccented notes on the snare, and baião or samba with the feet.
   - Add a snare rimshot on the note before the accented tom note.

3. Play accented notes as cymbal crashes along with bass drum, unaccented notes on the snare, and quarter notes on the hi-hat (LF).
   - Add a snare rimshot on the note before the cymbal crash.

4. Play all notes on various drums as fills, changing drums on accented notes. Play baião or samba with the feet.

LESSON 24

Phrases: Double Time

Here, we will compress the phrases and play them twice as fast (double time). The quarter note becomes an eighth and the eighth becomes a sixteenth. Since they are double time, you'll play them twice per bar. We'll use what is called "subtractive sticking." Play the right hand on notes falling on the eighth-note subdivisions in the bar (1, and, etc.) and the left hand on the off-beat sixteenth-note subdivisions (e, ah).

Here are the first eight phrases written out as examples. Play the rest of the exercises looking at the "Essential One-Bar Phrases" page. Once you're comfortable playing these on the practice pad, move on to the "Drum Set Applications."

Drum Set Applications

1. Play the exercises as fills around the drums over quarter notes on the bass drum.

2. Play the phrase on the bass drum, eighth notes on hi-hat (RH), and beats 2 and 4 on snare drum (LH).

3. Alternate phrase notes on the bass drum and snare (LH), and eighth notes on the hi-hat (RH).

4. Play the phrases on the hi-hat (RH), beats 1 and 3 on the bass drum, and beats 2 and 4 on the snare (LH).

Paradiddles: Four Types

Paradiddles are a useful building block, and you'll hear them everywhere in contemporary drumming. They are used in grooves, fills, and soloing. It's a super efficient way of getting around the kit.

Here, we take the paradiddle and play it four different ways by shifting the starting point one eighth note later each time. It gives the illusion of displacing the downbeat. The important part is to hold the downbeat with your right foot.

Be sure to start slowly, and make a broad dynamic difference between the accented notes (swing the stick all the way back) and unaccented notes (tap strokes that only raise one inch off the pad).

Play the rest of the exercises looking at the "Essential One-Bar Phrases" page. Once you're comfortable playing these on the practice pad, move on to the "Drum Set Applications."

Drum Set Applications

1. Play the exercises on the snare drum over baião or samba with the feet.

2. Play accented notes on the toms, unaccented notes on the snare, and baião or samba with the feet.

3. Play accented notes as cymbal crashes along with bass drum, unaccented notes on the snare, and half notes on the hi-hat (LF).

4. Play on the hi-hat (RH) and snare drum (LH), and beats 1 and 3 on the bass drum.

5. Play on the ride cymbal with accents on the bell (RH), snare drum (LH) and bass drum unison with the RH accents, and beats 1 and 3 on the hi-hat (LF).

Sixteenth Notes with Double Paradiddles on the Phrase Notes

Here, we will start a paradiddle on the phrase note and fill the remaining notes with double strokes. Note that after exercise 1, they alternate lead on the repeat.

Here are the first eight phrases written out as examples. Play the rest of the exercises looking at the "Essential One-Bar Phrases" page. Once you're comfortable playing these on the practice pad, move on to the "Drum Set Applications."

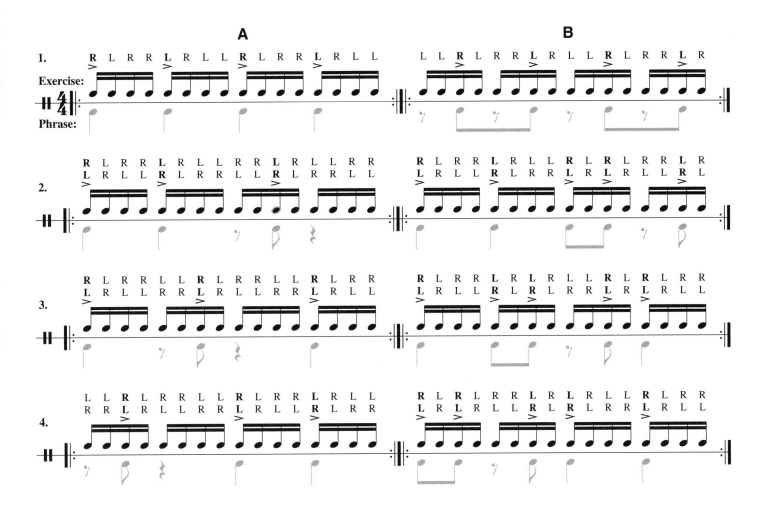

Drum Set Applications

1. Play the exercises on the snare drum over baião or samba with the feet.

2. Play with accented notes on the toms, unaccented notes on the snare, and baião or samba with the feet.

3. Play accented notes as cymbal crashes along with bass drum, unaccented notes on the snare, and quarter notes on the hi-hat (LF).

Sixteenth Notes with Flam Paradiddles and Flam Paradiddle-Diddles

This is a similar sticking pattern to the previous lesson with the addition of flams on the phrase notes. Remember to lift the stick up for the main stroke of the flam, and keep all the other strokes low to the pad. Once again, after exercise 1, we will alternate lead on the repeat.

Here are the first eight phrases written out as examples. Play the rest of the exercises looking at the "Essential One-Bar Phrases" page. Once you're comfortable playing these on the practice pad, move on to the "Drum Set Applications."

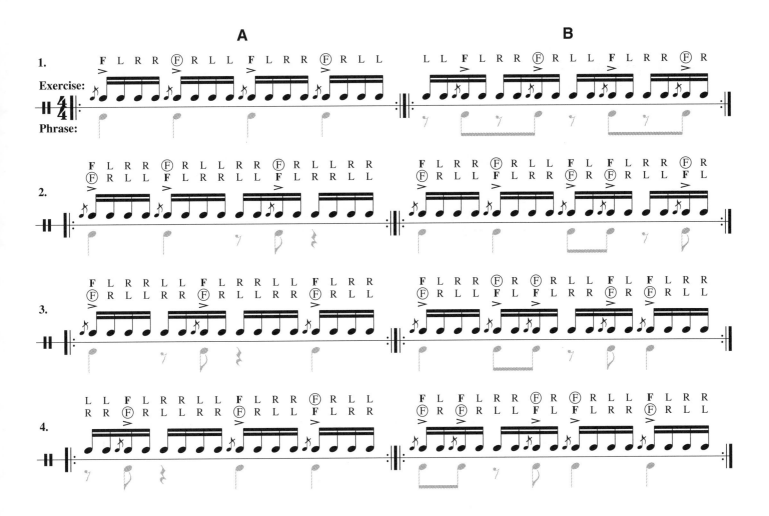

Drum Set Applications

1. Play the exercises on the snare over baião with the feet.

2. Play with primary flam notes on the toms, everything else on the snare, and baião or samba with the feet.

3. Play primary flam notes as cymbal crashes along with bass drum, everything else on the snare, and quarter notes on the hi-hat (LF).

Sixteenth Notes with Drag Paradiddles

Here's another paradiddle exercise with a drag on the phrase note. It's a phenomenal double-stroke workout. Try to keep the thirty-second notes nice and crisp. After exercise 1, these alternate lead on the repeat.

Here are the first eight phrases written out as examples. Play the rest of the exercises looking at the "Essential One-Bar Phrases" page. Once you're comfortable playing these on the practice pad, move on to the "Drum Set Applications."

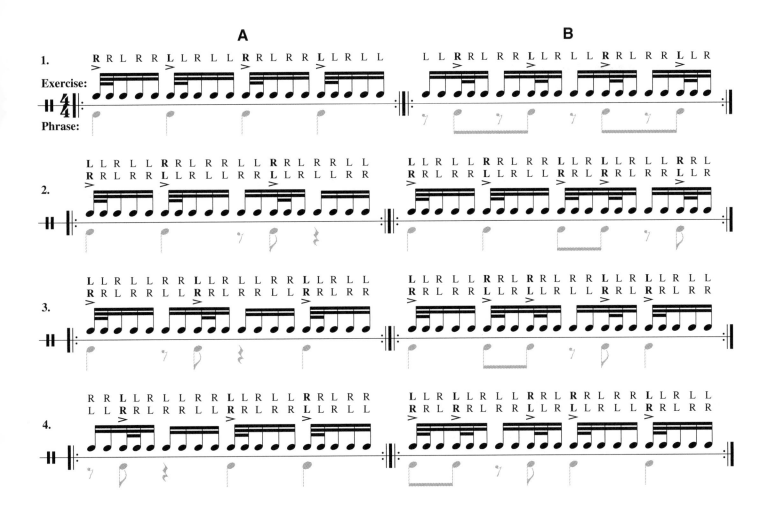

Drum Set Applications

1. Play the exercises on the snare over baião or samba with the feet.

2. Play the last two sixteenths before the accented note on toms, and
    baião or samba with the feet.

Flamtaps and Windmills

Here are two rudimental stickings that are great chops builders for getting around the kit.

FLAMTAP

A *flamtap* is a flam followed by a tap, just like it says in the title. What I like about the flamtap is it produces three taps in a row with each hand. It's a great workout. Be sure to start with the flam downstroke all the way up, and keep all the tap strokes low to the pad.

Play a flamtap when you see two eighth notes in a row.

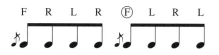

WINDMILL

Windmills function like a flamtap with two extra single strokes. Practice these very slowly until you are comfortable with them.

Practice these rudiments and get comfortable with the stickings before playing them within the phrase system.

Sixteenth Notes with Flamtaps and Windmills on the Phrases

Now, we will plug the flamtap and windmill into the phrase system. Whenever there is space of a quarter note or greater after a note, play the windmill. Eighth notes get the flamtap. Note that in the "A" exercises, there are distances greater than a quarter note between hits. Here, you will add another two single strokes. Like in the previous lesson, exercise 1 is either right or left lead; after that, they alternate on the repeat.

On the following page are the first eight phrases written out as examples. Play the rest of the exercises looking at the "Essential One-Bar Phrases" page. Once you're comfortable playing these on the practice pad, move on to the "Drum Set Applications."

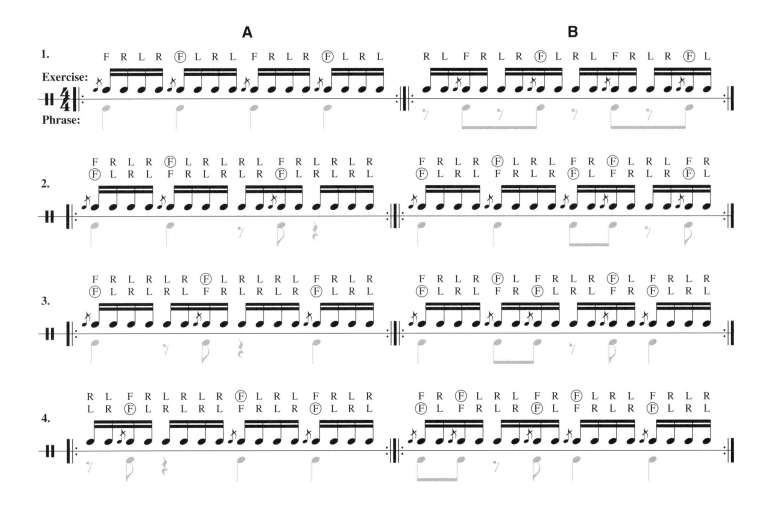

Drum Set Applications

1. Play the exercises on the snare drum over baião with the feet.

2. Play with primary flam notes on the toms, everything else on the snare drum, and baião or samba with the feet.

3. Play primary flam notes as crashes along with bass drum, everything else on the snare, and quarter notes on the hi-hat (LF).

LESSON 31

Playing Diddles on the Phrase Notes

In this exercise, we will continue filling in the sixteenths around the phrases, but now, we play two sixteenths with the right stick on every phrase note. It has the effect of fattening up the note. This technique sounds great on the kit as solo vocabulary or with right-hand ride and left-hand snare grooves.

This exercise uses the "A" phrases only.

Here are four phrases written out as examples. Play the rest of the exercises looking at the "Essential One-Bar Phrases" page. Once you're comfortable playing these on the practice pad, move on to the "Drum Set Applications."

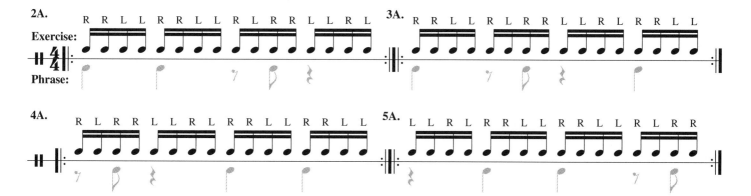

Drum Set Applications

1. Play the exercises on the snare drum over baião or samba with the feet.

2. Play the exercises on the toms (RH) and snare (LH), and baião or samba with the feet.

3. Play the exercises on the hi-hat (RH) and snare (LH), and baião or samba with the feet.

Sixteenths with Three Notes on a Long Phrase Note

In this exercise, we will play three consecutive notes in one hand whenever you see a phrase note that has more than an eighth note's space after it. This leads to great phrasing applications for jazz and Latin playing. Play exercise 1A, 1B, and after that, play only the B's.

Here are five phrases written out as examples. Play the rest of the exercises looking at the "Essential One-Bar Phrases" page. Once you're comfortable playing these on the practice pad, move on to the "Drum Set Applications."

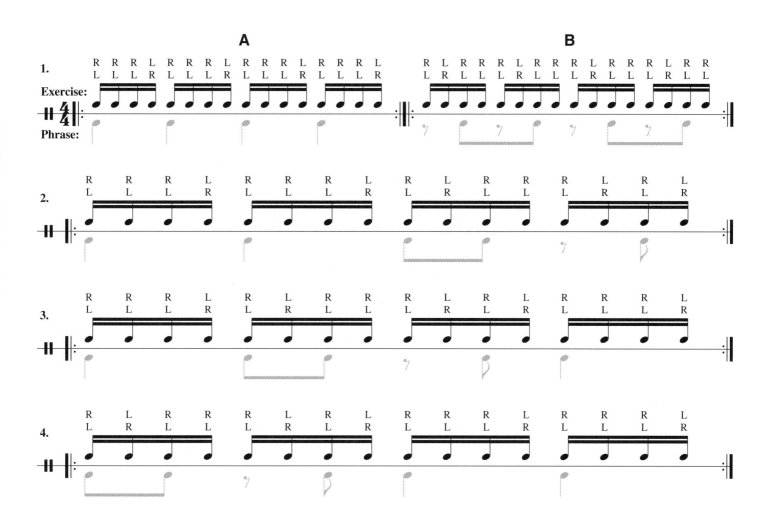

Drum Set Applications

1. Play the exercises on snare over baião or samba with the feet.

2. Play "R" notes on snare (LH) and ride (RH) in unison, and "L" notes on either bass drum or hi-hat.

3. Play "R" notes on snare (LH), "L" notes on bass drum (half time), jazz ride pattern on the ride cymbal (RH), and hi-hat on beats 2 and 4 (LF).

Consecutive Sixteenth Notes that Change on the Phrase Notes

This is an excellent exercise for building speed and fluidity. Here, we will repeat consecutive notes in one hand until getting to a phrase note, then change hands until the next phrase note. Strive for consistency and endurance, here. Try to float the stick away from your palm on the repeated notes. After exercise 1A and 1B, the stickings alternate on repeat.

Here are the first eight phrases written out as examples. Play the rest of the exercises looking at the "Essential One-Bar Phrases" page. Once you're comfortable playing these on the practice pad, move on to the "Drum Set Applications."

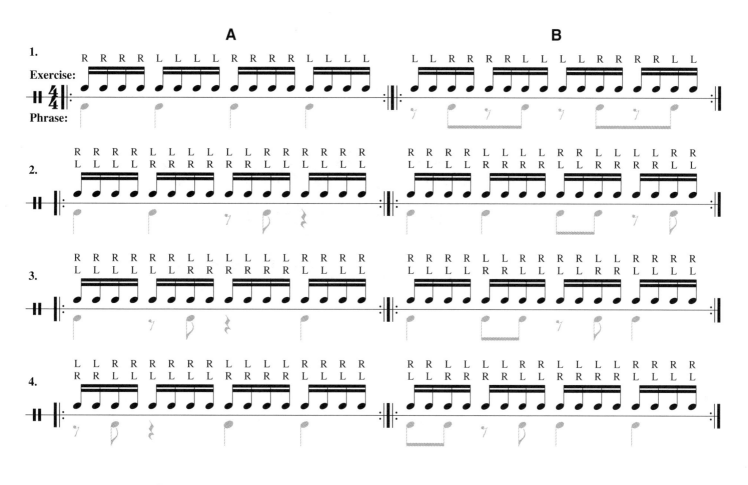

Drum Set Applications

1. Play the exercises on the snare over baião or samba with the feet.

2. Play the exercises on the floor tom (RH) and snare drum (LH), and baião or samba with the feet.

Doubling the Accented Sixteenths with Two Thirty-Second Notes

Speed blasts! These are great chops builders and they sound amazing as fills. Here, we double the sixteenth notes on the phrases so that they become thirty-second notes. Again, play exercise 1 with either right- or left-hand lead. Everything else alternates on the repeat.

Here are the first eight phrases written out as examples. Play the rest of the exercises looking at the "Essential One-Bar Phrases" page. Once you're comfortable playing these on the practice pad, move on to the "Drum Set Applications."

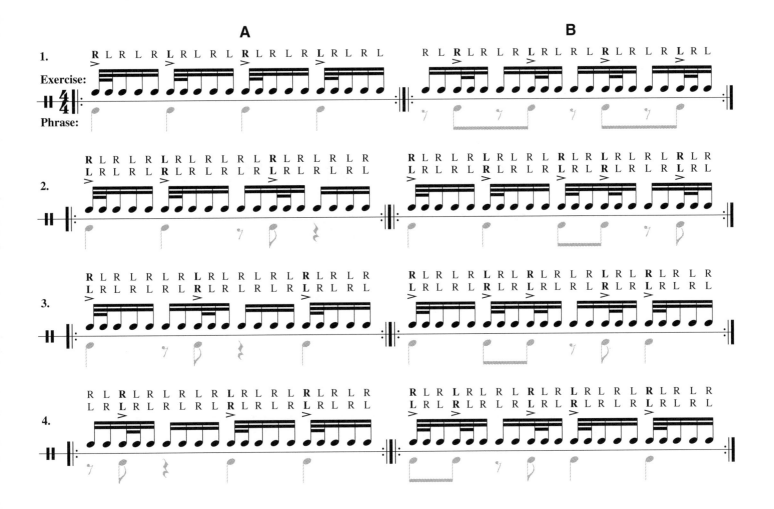

Drum Set Applications

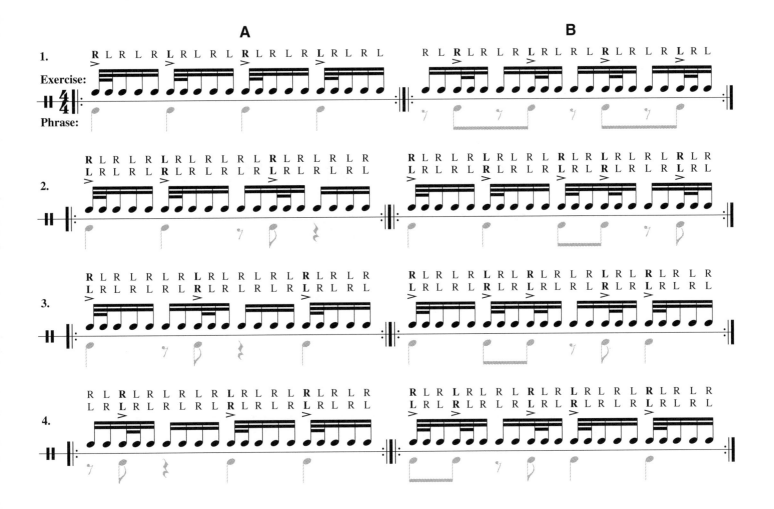

1. Play the exercises on the snare drum over baião or samba with the feet.

2. Play thirty-second notes on the toms, everything else on the snare, and baião or samba with the feet.

3. Play thirty-second notes on the hi-hat, everything else on the snare, and the phrase notes on bass drum.

4. Play all notes as fills, changing drums on the thirty-second notes.

Filling in Sixteenths on Funk Accents

FUNK PHRASING

Funk drumming has a strong sixteenth-note feel under the pulse. In *funk phrasing*, we're going to delay the off-beat eighth note so that it falls on the last sixteenth of the beat. We'll still read our "Essential One-Bar Phrases" page, but we'll play it with funk phrasing, like this:

Now, we'll get a feel for funk phrasing by filling in the sixteenths around the phrases. Note the stick height information over the stickings. We will snap the stick up the sixteenth before the next accent. Practice this very slowly at first, and really exaggerate the stick heights.

Here are the first eight phrases written out as examples. Play the rest of the exercises looking at the "Essential One-Bar Phrases" page. Once you're comfortable playing these on the practice pad, move on to the "Drum Set Applications."

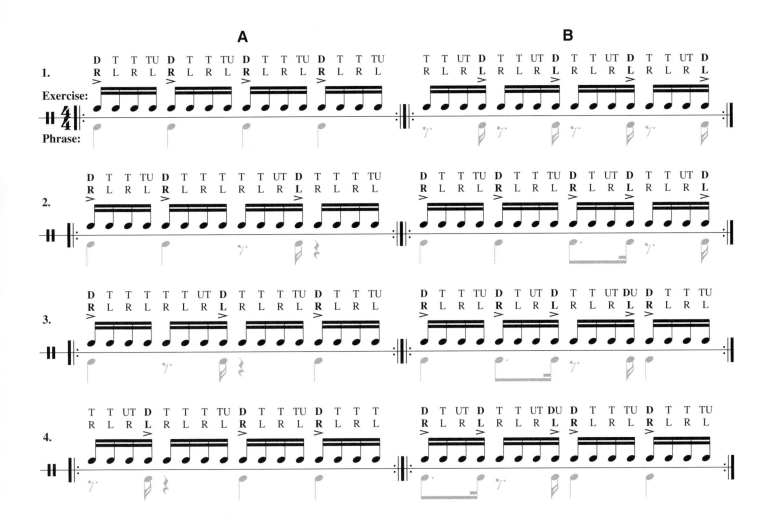

D: Downstroke, U: Upstroke, T: Tap. When two stroke indications appear together, they correspond to left and right hands.

Drum Set Applications

1. Play the exercises on the snare drum over baião or samba with the feet.

2. Play accented notes on the toms, unaccented notes on the snare drum, and baião or samba with the feet.
   - Play the snare drum note before the tom with a rimshot.

3. Play accented notes as cymbal crashes along with bass drum, unaccented notes on the snare, and quarter notes on the hi-hat (LF).
   - Play a rimshot snare note before the cymbal crash.

Flams on the Funk Accent

In this lesson, we'll continue with "Funk Phrasing" and add flams to the phrase notes. Notice that phrase 14 produces a rudiment called a "pataflafla."

Here are the first eight phrases written out as examples. Play the rest of the exercises looking at the "Essential One-Bar Phrases" page. Once you're comfortable playing these on the practice pad, move on to the "Drum Set Applications."

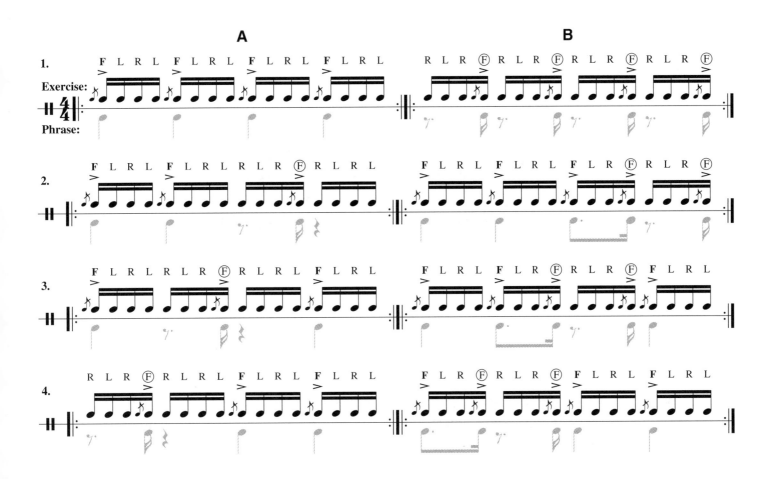

Drum Set Applications

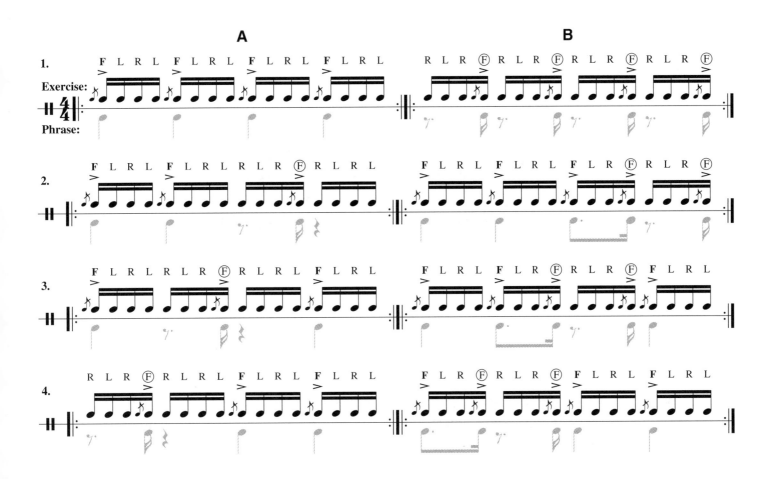

1. Play the exercises on the snare drum over baião or samba with the feet.

2. Play primary flam notes on the toms, everything else on the snare, and baião or samba with the feet.

3. Play primary flam notes as cymbal crashes along with bass drum, everything else on the snare, and quarter notes on the hi-hat (LF).

Paradiddles on the Funk Phrase Notes

This exercise uses two types of paradiddles to get around the funk phrase accents: one sticking for quarter notes and quarter rests, and another sticking for eighth notes on or off the beat.

On the following page are the first eight phrases written out as examples. Play the rest of the exercises looking at the "Essential One-Bar Phrases" page. Once you're comfortable playing these on the practice pad, move on to the "Drum Set Applications."

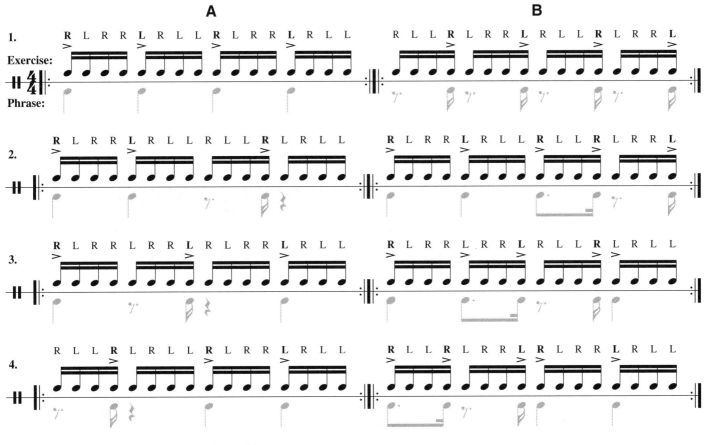

Drum Set Applications

1. Play the exercises on the snare drum over baião or samba with the feet.

2. Play accented notes on the toms, unaccented notes on the snare, and baião or samba with the feet.

3. Play accented notes as crashes along with bass drum, and quarter notes on the hi-hat (LF).

4. Play the exercises with right hand on hi-hat and left hand on snare drum. Play snare accents as rimshots (LH), and half notes on the bass drum.

5. Same as (4), with the bass drum playing along with hi-hat accents.

   a. Play the bass drum on the second of two consecutive hi-hat hits.

   b. Play the bass drum on the first of two consecutive hi-hat hits.

6. Same as (4), with bass drum playing unison with all right-hand hi-hat notes.

7. Same as (6), with quarter notes on the ride cymbal (RH).

8. Play the exercises with right hand on ride cymbal and left hand on snare drum. Play right-hand accents on the bell of the ride and left-hand accents on the snare drum. Play the bass drum unison with the right-hand accents.

LESSON 38

Sixteenth Notes with Five-Stroke Rolls Resolving on Funk Phrases: Double Strokes

Now, we'll insert a five-stroke roll into the mix so that it ends on a funk phrase note. We basically double the two sixteenths that come before the phrase note. These phrases work well as hi-hat fills in a funk context.

Here are the first eight phrases written out as examples. Play the rest of the exercises looking at the "Essential One-Bar Phrases" page. Once you're comfortable playing these on the practice pad, move on to the "Drum Set Applications."

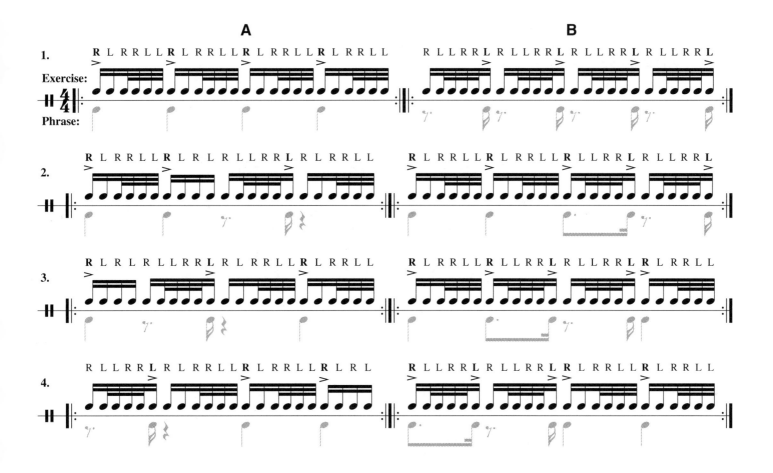

Drum Set Applications

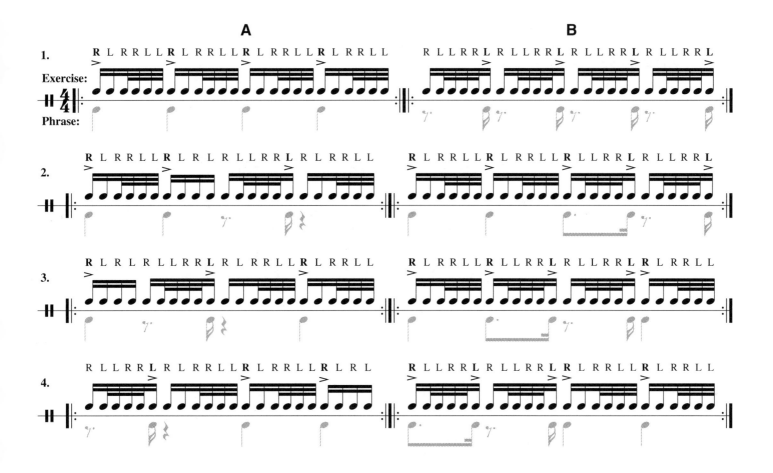

1. Play the exercises on the snare drum over baião or samba with the feet. ▶

2. Play accented notes on the toms, unaccented notes on the snare, and baião or samba with the feet. ▶

3. Play accented notes as cymbal crashes along with bass drum, unaccented notes on the snare, and quarter notes on the hi-hat (LF). ▶

4. Play the exercises on the hi-hat. Play the snare on the accents occurring on beats 2 and 4 or the sixteenth before (whichever the phrase dictates). Play the bass drum on beats 1 and 3. ▶

Sixteenth Notes with Five-Stroke Rolls Resolving on Funk Phrases: Alternating Strokes

In this exercise, we will once again double the two sixteenth notes that precede the funk phrase note producing a five-stroke roll. This time, we will use alternating strokes instead of diddles.

Here are the first eight phrases written out as examples. Play the rest of the exercises looking at the "Essential One-Bar Phrases" page. Once you're comfortable playing these on the practice pad, move on to the "Drum Set Applications."

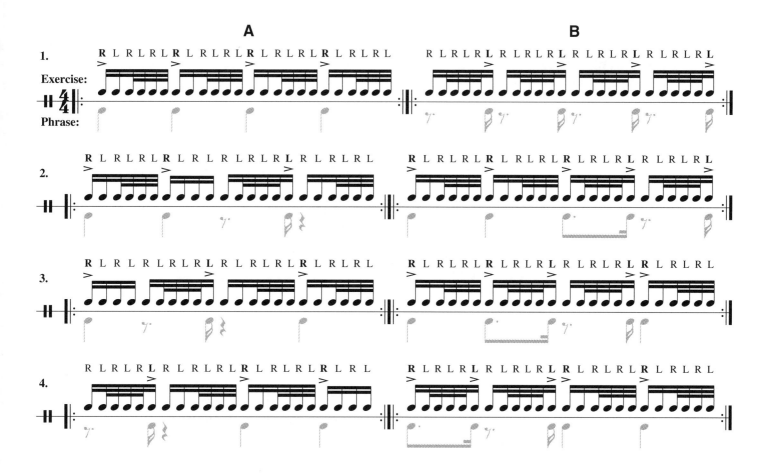

Drum Set Applications

1. Play the exercises on snare over baião or samba with the feet.

2. Play accented notes on the toms, unaccented notes on the snare, and baião or samba with the feet.

3. Play accented notes as cymbal crashes along with bass drum, unaccented notes on the snare, and quarter notes on the hi-hat (LF).

4. Play the exercises on the hi-hat. Play the snare on the accents occurring on beats 2 and 4 or the sixteenth before (whichever the phrase dictates). Play the bass drum on beats 1 and 3.

Doubling the Unaccented Sixteenths on Funk Phrases Using Double Strokes

Here's a real workout for the double-stroke roll. We'll double all of the unaccented sixteenths with double strokes and end on the funk phrases. Strive for consistency and endurance.

Here are the first eight phrases written out as examples. Play the rest of the exercises looking at the "Essential One-Bar Phrases" page. Once you're comfortable playing these on the practice pad, move on to the "Drum Set Applications."

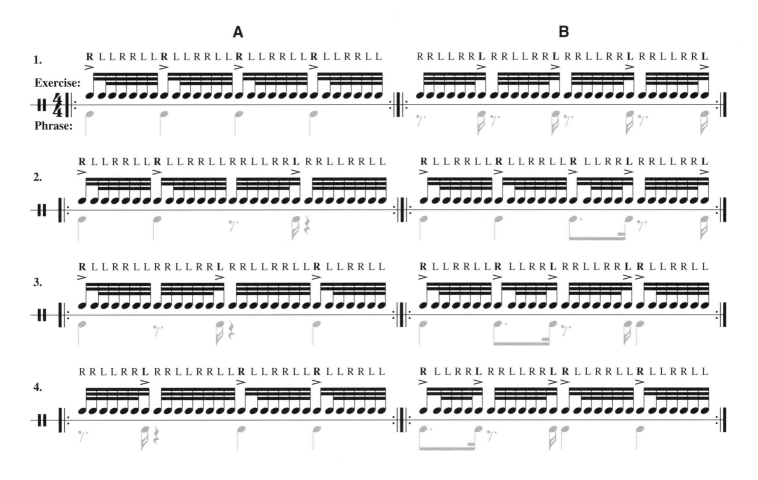

Drum Set Applications

1. Play the exercises on the snare drum over baião or samba with the feet.

2. Play accented notes on the toms, unaccented notes on the snare, and baião or samba with the feet.

3. Play accented notes as cymbal crashes along with bass drum, unaccented notes on the snare, and quarter notes on the hi-hat (LF).

Doubling the Unaccented Sixteenths on Funk Phrases: Alternating Sticking

This single-stroke exercise will build serious chops. Alternate all the way through this lesson; after exercise 1, you will switch leads on the repeat. Pop the accent so the phrase keeps its rhythmic shape.

Here are the first eight phrases written out as examples. Play the rest of the exercises looking at the "Essential One-Bar Phrases" page. Once you're comfortable playing these on the practice pad, move on to the "Drum Set Applications."

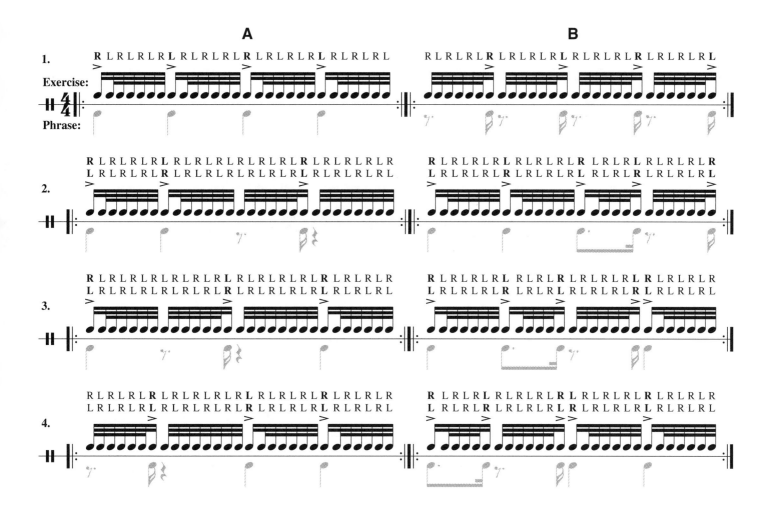

Drum Set Applications

1. Play the exercises on the snare drum over baião or samba with the feet.

2. Play accented notes on the toms, unaccented notes on the snare drum, and baião or samba with the feet.

3. Play accented notes as cymbal crashes along with bass drum, unaccented notes on the snare, and quarter notes on the hi-hat (LF).

LESSON 42

Six Notes per Beat, Accent on Phrase Note

Sextuplets on each quarter note give a densely packed jazzy feel. The phrase notes return to their natural position, either on the beat or on the eighth note.

Here are the first eight phrases written out as examples. Play the rest of the exercises looking at the "Essential One-Bar Phrases" page. Once you're comfortable playing these on the practice pad, move on to the "Drum Set Applications."

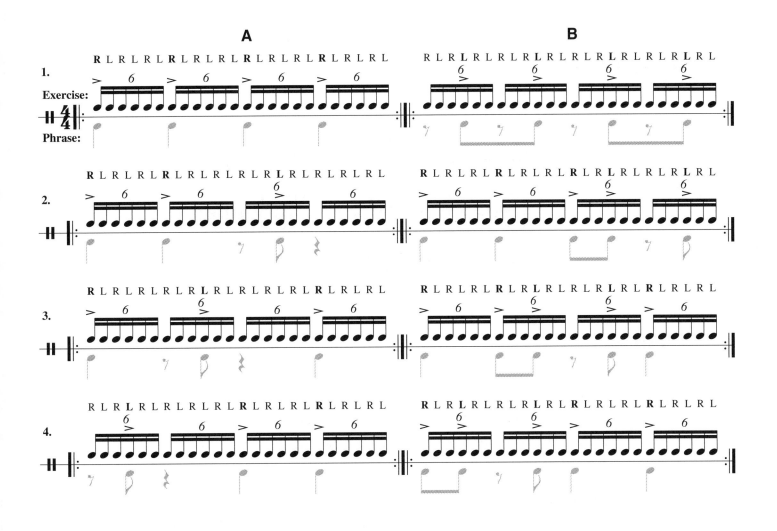

Drum Set Applications

1. Play the exercises on the snare drum over baião or samba with the feet.

2. Play accented notes on the toms, unaccented notes on the snare, and baião or samba with the feet.

3. Play accented notes as cymbal crashes along with bass drum, unaccented notes on the snare, and quarter notes on the hi-hat (LF).

4. Play all the notes on various drums (as fills), changing drums on each accent.

Six Notes per Beat (Sextuplets), Diddle on the Phrase Note

This exercise is a fun workout. Here, we have six notes in the space of a quarter note. There is a *diddle* (**R**LL or **L**RR) on the phrase note with alternating strokes filling in the rest of the measure. After exercise 1, this exercise wraps around and alternates leading hand on the repeats.

Of course, we want repetition (repetition, repetition, repetition). Here are the first eight phrases written out as examples. Play the rest of the exercises looking at the "Essential One-Bar Phrases" page. Once you're comfortable playing these on the practice pad, move on to the "Drum Set Applications."

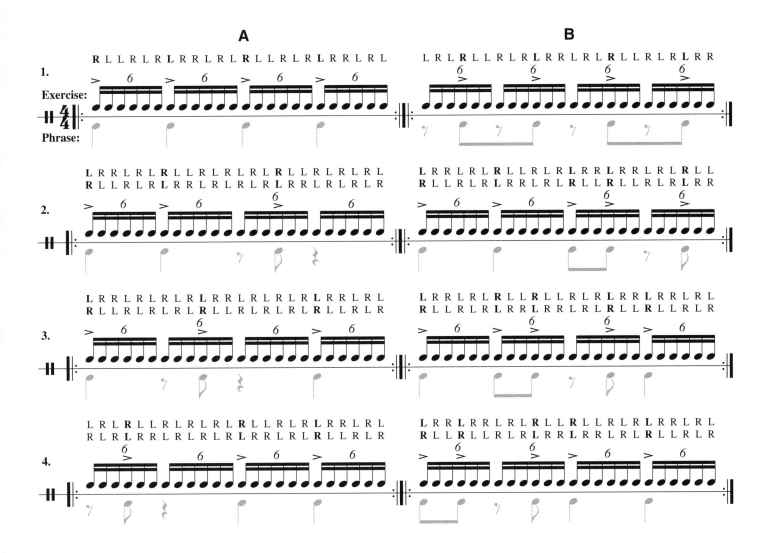

Drum Set Applications

1. Play the exercises on the snare drum over baião or samba with the feet.

2. Play accented notes on the toms, unaccented notes on the snare, and with baião or samba in the feet.

3. Play accented notes as cymbal crashes along with bass drum, unaccented notes on the snare, and quarter notes on the hi-hat (LF).

Paradiddle-Diddles

The paradiddle-diddle is like the cousin to the paradiddle. It's the same phrase with an added double stroke. The paradiddle-diddle is a great way to group sticking information into useful musical phrases. These are super common in jazz drumming.

There are six varieties (or permutations) of the paradiddle-diddle. Actually, they are all the same sticking, except they start in different places in the pattern.

- Tap your foot on the first note of the pattern to keep track of the downbeat.

- Don't forget to swing the stick back on the accents, and play the unaccented notes as tap strokes.

Here are the six varieties of paradiddle-diddles written out, with quarter notes on beats 1 and 3. Tap your foot on these notes to keep track of the downbeat.

Drum Set Applications

1. Play the exercises on the snare drum over baião with the feet. Swing the eighth notes.

2. Play accented notes on the toms, unaccented notes on the snare, and baião in the feet.

3. Play accented notes as cymbal crashes along with bass drum, unaccented notes on the snare, and quarter notes on the hi-hat (LF).

4. Play "R" notes on bass drum, "L" on snare drum, jazz ride cymbal (RH), and beats 2 and 4 on hi-hat (LF).

LESSON 45

Paradiddle-Diddles around the Phrases

Here's how the paradiddle-diddles work plugged into the phrase page. Notice how the left-hand accent falls on the last sixteenth-note triplet of the beat.

These are the first eight phrases written out as examples. Play the rest of the exercises looking at the "Essential One-Bar Phrases" page. Once you're comfortable playing these on the practice pad, move on to the "Drum Set Applications."

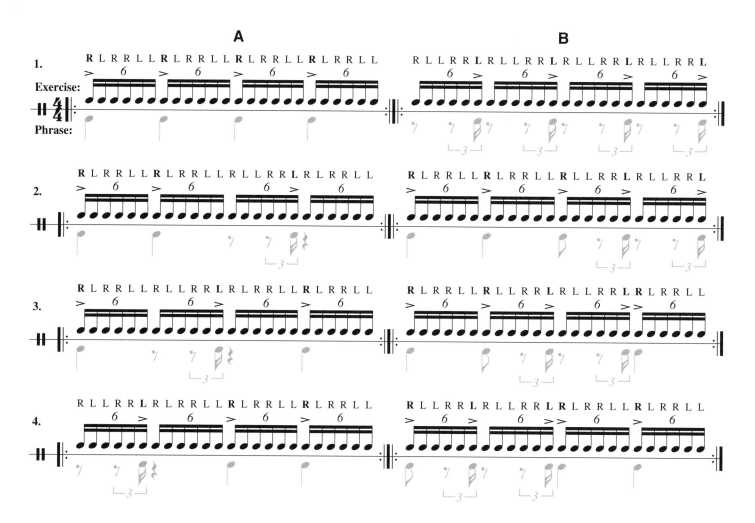

Drum Set Applications

1. Play the exercises on the snare drum over baião with the feet. Swing the eighth notes.

2. Play accented notes on the toms, unaccented notes on the snare drum, and baião with the feet.

3. Play accented notes as cymbal crashes along with bass drum, unaccented notes on the snare, and quarter notes on the hi-hat (LF).

4. Play "R" notes on hi-hat, "L" notes on snare, accents that are close to beats 2 and 4 on the snare, and remaining accents on bass drum.

5. Play "R" notes on the ride cymbal, with accents on the bell, and "L" notes on hi-hat with accents on the snare drum. Play the bass drum unison with the right-hand accents.

PHRASES WITH PARADIDDLE-DIDDLES

This exercise uses two paradiddle-diddle stickings and plugs them into the phrases. The effect of the paradiddle-diddle is to move the off-beat eighth note to the last partial of the sextuplet. It works like this:

Sextuplets with Three Consecutive Notes on a Long Phrase Note

In this exercise, we will play three consecutive notes in one hand whenever there is a phrase note with more than an eighth note's space after it. Play each exercise starting with either the right or left hand. These sound great on the kit, in a jazz context. After 1A and 1B, play only the "B" phrases for this exercise.

Here are the first five phrases written out as examples. Play the rest of the exercises looking at the "Essential One-Bar Phrases" page. Once you're comfortable playing these on the practice pad, move on to the "Drum Set Applications."

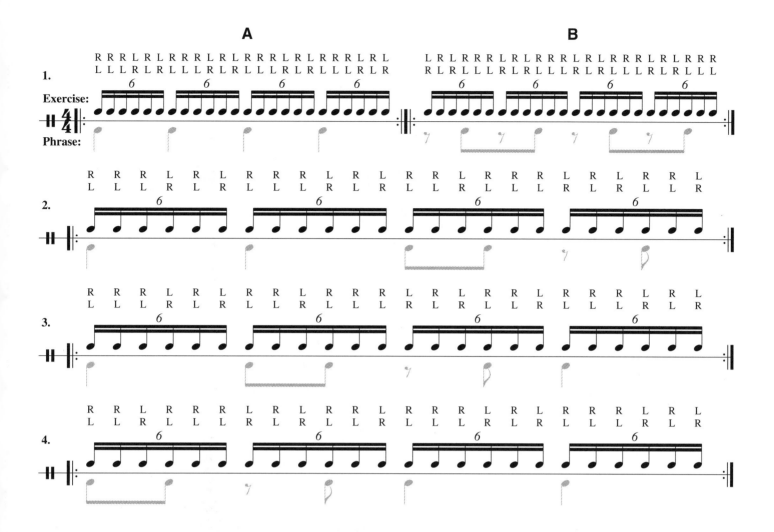

Drum Set Applications

1. Play the exercises on the snare over baião with the feet. Swing the eighth notes.

Play half time with "R" notes on the snare drum, "L" notes on the bass drum, jazz ride pattern on the ride cymbal (RH), and hi-hat on 2 and 4.

LESSON 47

Swiss Triplets: Three Types

Here, we will explore the three options for playing the Swiss triplet. It's the same sticking permutated three times. Keep your foot solid on the downbeats to keep track of where you are. Once you're comfortable playing these on the practice pad, move on to the "Drum Set Applications."

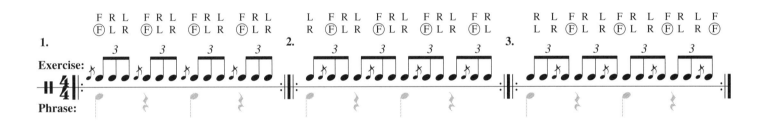

Drum Set Applications

1. Play the exercises on the snare over baião with the feet. Swing the eighth notes. ▣

2. Play the primary flam notes on the toms, everything else on snare, and baião with the feet. ▣
   • Play the note before the flam on the tom. ▣

3. Play primary flam notes as cymbal crashes along with bass drum, everything else on the snare, and quarter notes on the hi-hat (LF). ▣
   • Play the note before the flam on the tom.

LESSON 48

Swiss Triplets and Six-Stroke Windmills

This is another exercise where we play six notes per beat. We are going to use two closely related rudiments that show up a lot in jazz drumming.

SWISS TRIPLETS

Here again is the Swiss triplet rudiment. Play this slowly at first. It's important that the downstroke of the flam ends close to the pad so that the next tap stroke is soft.

F = Right-Hand Flam

Ⓕ= Left-Hand Flam

SIX-STROKE WINDMILL

This six-stroke windmill is the extended version of the Swiss triplet. Three alternating notes make it a six-note phrase. Note that in lesson 49, there are also a few phrases that add another three notes to make it a nine-note phrase.

Practice the six-stroke windmill on a pad before plugging it into the phrase system.

Swiss Triplets and Six-Stroke Windmills on the Phrases

Now, we'll plug the Swiss triplet and six-stroke windmill into the "Phrase Page." Here, we fill the measure with sixteenth-note triplets and play a flam on the phrase note. Once you get familiar with these, go ahead and play the whole phrase page from top to bottom without stopping. Play each at least eight times, and then go on to the next. This exercise switches lead every other repetition (except for 1a and 1b).

Here are the first eight phrases written out as examples. Play the rest of the exercises looking at the "Essential One-Bar Phrases" page. Once you're comfortable playing these on the practice pad, move on to the "Drum Set Applications."

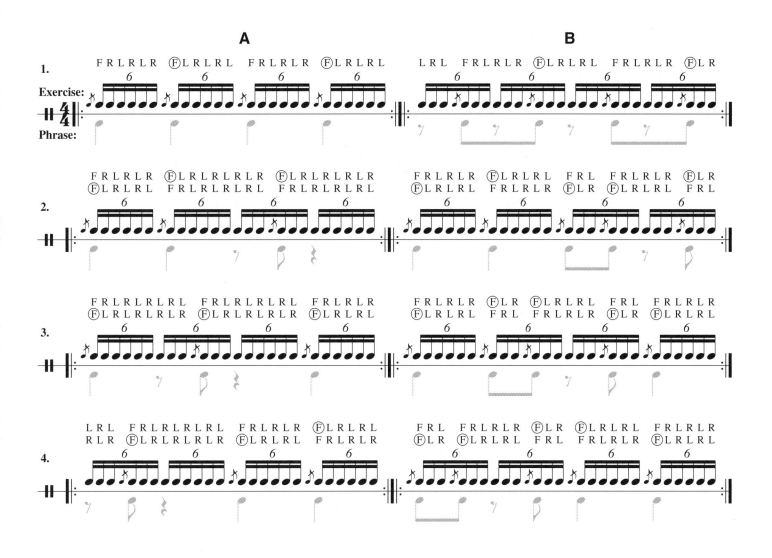

Drum Set Applications

1. Play the exercises on the snare drum over baião with the feet.

2. Play primary flam notes on the toms, everything else on snare, and baião with the feet.

3. Play primary flam notes as cymbal crashes along with bass drum, everything else on the snare, and quarter notes on the hi-hat (LF).

Doubling the Accented Sextuplet Phrase Notes

More thirty-second-note blasts! Here, we will play two thirty-second notes on every phrase note. These exercises alternate all the way through. They all (except 1A and 1B) change lead every other repetition. These are super effective chop-builders and sound great as tom fills on the kit. Try to finish the whole phrase page in one sitting.

Here are the first eight phrases written out as examples. Play the rest of the exercises looking at the "Essential One-Bar Phrases" page. Once you're comfortable playing these on the practice pad, move on to the "Drum Set Applications."

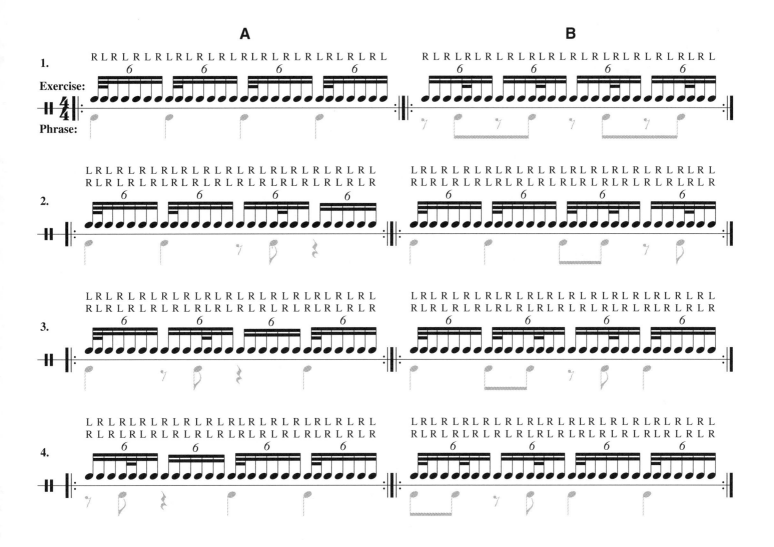

Drum Set Applications

1. Play the exercises on the snare drum over baião or samba with the feet.

2. Play thirty-second notes on the toms and everything else on the snare drum.

3. Play the exercise on various drums as fills, changing drums on the thirty-second notes.

APPENDIX

Phrases with Three Grooves

PHRASES WITH BAIÃO GROOVE

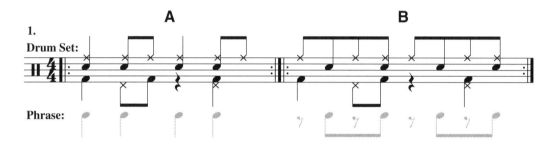

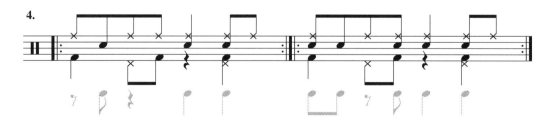

PHRASES WITH SAMBA GROOVE

A   **B**

7.
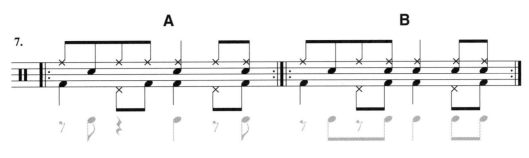

8.

9.
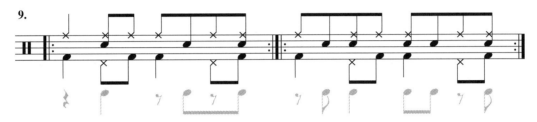

10.   12.

11.   13.
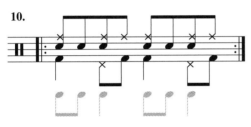   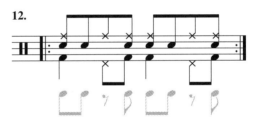

14.

PHRASES WITH JAZZ RIDE

ABOUT THE AUTHOR

Russ Gold's performing experience includes work with musicians as diverse as Gary Lyons (producer of Rolling Stones, Grateful Dead), Johnny Colla of Huey Lewis and the News, Seth Justman of the J. Giles Band, and jazz greats Tom Scott, Sam Rivers, George Coleman, Dave Douglas, Vinx, and Howard Johnson. He has toured extensively throughout the United States, Europe, Africa, and Asia, performing with jazz, rock, fusion, and acclaimed musicals *Wicked*, *Jersey Boys*, and *Rent*. He has earned endorsements of Sabian cymbals, ProMark sticks, Fishman transducers, and Kurzweil synthesizers. Visit www.russgold.com to view a detailed list of concerts and recording credits.

STUDY MUSIC
with
BERKLEE ONLINE

Study Berklee's curriculum, with Berklee faculty members, in a collaborative online community. Transform your skill set and find your inspiration in all areas of music, from songwriting and music production, to music business, theory, orchestration, and everything in between. Build lifelong relationships with like-minded students on your own time, from anywhere in the world.

Discover Your Own Path at
Berkleemusic.com

Learn On Your Own, But Never By Yourself